Power, Race, and Culture

The Evolution of a Black Anthropologist

Janis Faye Hutchinson

Hamilton Books
A member of
The Rowman & Littlefield Publishing Group, Inc.
Lanham · Boulder · New York · Toronto · Oxford

Copyright © 2005 by
Hamilton Books
4501 Forbes Boulevard
Suite 200
Lanham, Maryland 20706
UPA Acquisitions Department (301) 459-3366

PO Box 317
Oxford
OX2 9RU, UK

Library of Congress Control Number: 2005921423
ISBN   978-0-7618-3136-5

This book is dedicated to

The People of Birmingham

Table of Contents

Preface

A Collision Course

As an African American female growing up in Birmingham during the Civil Rights period, I have always had a strong consciousness about race and racism. The segregated environment, after all, had been the norm since the end of slavery, imposing race as the most important criteria of a person's existence. Race determined occupation, income, standard of living, success or failure, as well as the type and quality of social interactions and relationships. Invincible, invasive, this measure of humans has touched innumerable lives.

Regardless of class, all Blacks had to use the **COLORED ONLY** restroom, had to drink from **COLORED ONLY** water fountains, had to attend separate schools, and had to eat in the basement (where actually, the best food was served) at Woolworth. We lived like refugees in a prison camp, and indeed we were prisoners of racism. While slave passbooks were no longer required by law, we had indicators that maintained the law of separation—segregation.

Needless to say, power and history have exacted an incalculable and inescapable price on a people charged with living under a hostile and oppressive system such as one where race supplants character or any other impartial measure of man. Wounds have been slow to heal, if at all. This was never truer for me than three occurrences of which I was intricately involved. These situations were tightly bound around my professional, as well as my intra- and interpersonal lives, and each one impacted this project in particular ways.

Quite surprisingly, reality bit me in the butt—as it has been prone to do to quite a number of people, in general. The nip began when as a professor of anthropology, I developed a course on *Race and Anthropology* at the University of Houston where I looked at the concept of race from a historical perspective. That Europeans were superior, representing the highest stage of man's development, and therefore, had a natural or inherent right to dominate so-called inferior cultures was a position that reigned from the sixteenth to the nineteenth centuries as anthropology's mainstay of evolutionary theories of man. That was not a news flash to me. And even if so, this and other theories of White supremacy like it, however, were debunked (found not to be true or factual) from around the mid to late nineteen hundreds, replaced by evidence that all societies did develop along the same path toward *Homo sapiens*; hence, terms such as inferior or superior were inapplicable designations. Anthropologists may disagree on a lot of things, but our human origin is not one of them.

Nevertheless, the stage on which White race superiority versus Black race inferiority was hammered home repeatedly had been built on a Machiavellian ("might makes right") foundation. Those with power (gained by hook, crook, the bible, and a gun) ruled over those who had never even heard of shoestrings, less known had any. The poisonous message seeped into all aspects of culture, in every facet of living, spoiling everything and everyone it touched in America. Accordingly, the empowered also held a strong grasp over historical events, sometimes setting things up to happen that might not have without interference or deliberate expansion (which we considered history), his-story. And his-story painted us humanly unworthy. Consequently, the color of our complexion colored the nature of our relationships, not just between us, but also with others of different ethnicities.

My sojourn into history triggered the memory of my days as a youth. I remembered wanting to know why I couldn't go to the Alabama Theater to see "Cinderella," attend any school I wanted to, or shop or eat anywhere I pleased. When I was around seven years old, we drove all day, at least it seemed like that, to go to an amusement park. Once we arrived, the White guy told us that they did not allow Negroes in the park. Consequently, at a very early age I learned that Whites treated Blacks differently simply because of skin tone, and it later occurred to me that Blacks, too, treated one another differently for the same reason.

Nevertheless, when teaching about race and racism, I did not capitalize on my past experiences in Birmingham to help explain how power and history interplayed in defining Black-White race relations, as we know it today. While my memory has dimmed on a number of things about my youth, instances and situations that could highlight the distant familiarity the students may have already possessed remained clear and bright in my mind. Yet, I didn't enlighten them; even though, my research into the early developments of the race concept in Europe revealed stereotypes that were created to justify the seizure of land and enslavement of people that remained in existence today! I had grown up stereotypically typecast as inferior, in a place, Birmingham, Alabama, that didn't seem as far away from Europe, after all.

More recently, a discussion about Ebonics on the Internet proved that this racist thinking had not changed. A woman claimed quite sincerely that Blacks spoke Ebonics because their mouths couldn't make certain sounds for the English language. Like her sixteenth century forbearers, she assumed biology was the reason for linguistic diversity.

This assumption, I knew, was shared widely across the country, and held by some of my students, as well. Still, my lips remained sealed, as if reprimanded by guilt and shame on what I knew intimately about racism. I decided to wait for the appropriate time, all the while knowing that a fitting occasion would never arise if I didn't allow it.

What I found informationally in support of my classroom lectures dovetailed into my social involvement with a former student and fellow anthropologist. Her name was Rebecca, (not her real name) and she was White. We were around the same age, and she, like me, came from a southern town. With a conscious effort, we met to talk about work and what was happening in our lives over lunch. It must be mentioned that although we lived in the same city, our social paths rarely crossed. This, of course, was not unusual despite the fact that integration has been around for quite some time. Goodness-gracious, residential areas in the United States were still basically segregated. Blacks tended to hang out with other Blacks and Whites being larger in number, at least in the United States, surrounded themselves with other Whites. Both represent and contribute to what takes place every Sunday morning, the most segregated time in America as Whites attend their churches, and other ethnic groups went to theirs — religious segregation.

Nevertheless, our luncheon meetings inevitably included discussions of race. While race was an issue in dealing with the larger community (Whites), the matter of colorism plagued the Black community. I had but to literally look in the mirror at my continued unwillingness to discuss my life in Birmingham to know how true this was for me. Looking at my family, for example, where we were as varied in skin color as we were in personality. I often wondered why my brother was very dark and I lighter complected, although I knew we had the same mother and father. Blacks thought of and treated light-skinned individuals differently from dark-skinned people. Light-skinned Blacks were thought to have more opportunity, to be better off economically, and to be physically more attractive. Later, I realized this is internalized racism, but at the time it was simply a part of life. This aspect of Black life has been detrimental for people trying to live up (or down) to expectations. For instance, a guy in my neighborhood was very light-skinned with straight Black hair. If you did not know him or his family, you would have thought he was White. Because of his appearance, other Blacks gave him a hard time since they felt he could "pass" and therefore had more opportunity. He joined a tough group of Black guys and was eventually killed in a fight. At that time everyone felt that it was his skin color that killed him.

Today, the average person has come to consider skin color as the "right" criteria for defining "classic" race. While anthropologists have attempted to diverge from the concept of race, it still permeates their work. The importance of race has been such a significant bastion in society for so long that it has become impossible to ignore. Everyone is classified into a racial group and people think in terms of races because we have racial identities: identity is the way in which we think about ourselves, the cognitive structure that gives 'self' unity and social relatedness. The product of learning about 'self', while learning one's culture has been through racial identities.

This issue of race, I should also add, has been a difficult one for the field of anthropology to grasp concretely and to form a consensus. Even now, a new assessment of race and racial diversity has emerged, with current thinking that denies the existence of races, focusing instead on populations. Rebecca and I, however, knew full well—or at least, believed based upon our personal experiences—that race wasn't that easily explained, science or no science. Race was personal to us.

I suggested to her that we put our conversations on paper, linking our personal pasts with our professional insights. Thus, this book began as a collaborative project. We set out to write about our peculiar experiences growing up in the south during the Civil Rights era from the perspectives of a White female from Mississippi and an African American female from Alabama, who were both biological anthropologists.

From the beginning problems writing about our family perspectives on race arose. We were immensely fearful of offending them, and that's putting it mildly. Apprehensions of appearing racist and showing her family as such plagued Rebecca once she began recounting her experiences. There were also job considerations. She was finishing her dissertation at another university and would soon be on the job market: concerns that any presentation of a racist attitude on her part could hinder her job opportunities were real. When we received feedback from agents, they commented on the lack of depth in her sections. One said that it sounded as if she was holding back. When I talked to her about it, she replied that she was holding back because it would have been too painful to say more. At that point, she decided to withdraw from the project because she said she couldn't put any more energy into it. She wasn't willing to bear her soul and was afraid of looking like a racist. These things are understandable, and we have remained friends. Still, at that point, I was in a quandary about what to do.

A new graduate student, Joan, (again, an alias) came into my office one day to talk about a thesis topic. She too, was interested in race and racism in terms of White women. Well, I thought she might be interested in my project. Joan talked about her family, especially her mother. Like my previous collaborator and myself, it seemed that she too wanted to deal with some demons.

I have come to realize that we all reach a point in our lives when we want to deal with our past; in other words, shake the tree to see what falls. Introspection has been known to occur when one enters into her/his forties and feel more secure in and with 'self.' I sincerely hoped Joan would be willing to take the initial steps vital to personal growth.

When I approached her about the idea, she was instantly interested in participating in such a project. It dovetailed nicely with her thesis work, and she thought she had a family situation that would provide a unique White perspective. Exploring how her family's move to the South in the 1960s, when she was 12 years old, signaled a change in the trajectory of all their lives, and in particular, her mother's, she believed would be fascinating.

She always had this view of her mother as an egalitarian thinker who slowly converted to a bitterly racist posture after moving to the South, in allegiance to her stepfather, and perhaps as a result of the unrest generated by the Civil Rights movement. That was before taking on this project. But as she combed through the literature for her thesis and worked on this text, she began to uncover truths about her upbringing. It was as if she had discovered an old and battered trunk in the dark corner of the attic, where she lifted away layer by layer the more recent and stylish accouterment that covered the shameful, mildewed, impoverished garments of her family's social and psychological reality. She realized that for all her rhetoric of equality during her early childhood, her mother had not changed when she moved south, but rather had entered an environment that encouraged the flowering of her germinating racism. Her step-dad, a native Texan, who had always been more openly racist than her mother, also emerged from a cocoon of military-enforced tolerance into full and pernicious racist expression.

The South did not make her parents racist, as she had thought earlier. It simply provided the environment in which her parents' dormant racism could comfortably express itself. Joan's parents were quite successful by their own definition, but their success was achieved through unacknowledged entitlements and a gratuitous civil service system, in addition to a lifetime of backbreaking, relationship-destroying work.

As she worked on this project, she felt at times that she was betraying them and their hard work, especially considering all their efforts to build a life. She could easily recognize the sexism in her family, and through the writing of this project, she began to bring the racism into clear focus. Joan told me that when she took her first college course in her twenties (she's in her forties now) and immersed herself in the country's racial past, she assumed the mantle of collective guilt. She felt personally responsible for slavery. She wanted to understand how this country with its rhetoric of freedom could have legalized slavery just a hundred years ago. Finally, it was too much and she let the guilt slip away as she went on with her troubled White life in a protected White suburb. She walked away from the worry, justifying and rationalizing, "I can't change everything by myself; it's too confusing to understand; nobody listens anyway."

She could walk away, push the thoughts aside, turn her head from racial issues, try to ignore racism and live her life. That's part of what it has meant to be White. Whether they recognize it or not, they too are as ensnared in the same vicious web of racism as Blacks.

Writing this book has been gut-wrenching for all of us. As Joan re-thought her life and origins, she slipped into a depressive paralysis. Guilt-ridden, ashamed of who she had come from and aware that she felt such shame, Joan awakened in the middle of many nights, obsessing about what would happen if her mother read the book. She struggled through hours of sleeplessness, in anguish over the quality of her writing, burdening herself with the belief that this book would be so controversial that only superb writing could rescue it and her from infamy. She was further inhibited by the increasing realization that even her early childhood had been racist, that her whole nuclear family system, always admittedly dysfunctional, was corrupt, and that she had committed unwitting racist acts and unconsciously harbored racist thoughts, not just occasionally but fairly consistently throughout her life.

The book became impossible to complete. She wanted to hide from herself and her past, letting this project fall into some secret hidden place because it was too hard, too painful, and too thankless to continue. What good would it serve? Joan could see no way that publishing admissions of personal, familial, and institutional racism would ever do any good for her or anybody else. On the other hand, she had a conviction that things needed to be said out loud, needed to be printed and recognized as an American experience. But, she could not proceed and wished me well. I continued carrying the ghosts of a community experience.

I have been unable to walk away just because the pain of my individual history was too much to bear. Our collective history over time in America was even more wretched, as the rhetoric of our dehumanization was empowered by the systematic elimination of our traditions, the substitution of our language, and the destruction of our culture even as they denied us theirs. With this book, I hope to step out of the silence and into discourse. I hope the readers will step with me and begin their own search for the truths in their lives. My readings on the history of the race concept, training in biological anthropology, and growing up in the south during the Civil Rights period provide a unique context for the present discussion on race.

This discussion was stimulated by numerous conversations with Margie Walker. I want to thank Margie for her hard work in the production of this manuscript. Thank you for your questions, motivation, and commitment to the completion of this project.

Chapter One

Magic and Mayhem

"My beginnings have had a lasting affect on my life"

By the time I was born, Birmingham, Alabama was already a conflict-laden soap opera, replete with violent episodes and a cast in flux, spanning the issues from employment to education, and just because. The dramatists included mine and steel workers striking in protest of dangerous working conditions in jobs aspired for by strikebreakers and an actively powerful and combative KKK. The plot thickened when the stock characters began to wage a battle for freedom and equality, made even more gripping by the twisted perception that outside agitators had hailed upon their Magic City to disrupt their contented Black community. There were so many bombings that in 1963 a New York Times reporter called the city "Bombingham." Demands for civil rights, political rights and human rights made for a long-running volatile series in 'Bombingham,' a testament to the resiliency and adaptation of a culture stricken by power and history.

When the sun went down and the night awakened, feelings of promise, hope, and delight are evoked when you look down on the City of Birmingham. In fact, my hometown was called the 'Magic City' because downtown resided in a valley surrounded by hills, so that when the celestial lights twinkled at twilight and co-mingled with the dazzling array of home lights, one got this incredible sense of a magical place to behold — at night. The illusion ended with mornings, for in the harsh reality of daylight, Birmingham wore its very ethnocentric, White-southern-heritage, hate-face.

The White Citizens Council (a group of white businessmen) sanctioned violence and controlled the politics in the city. When the NAACP was banned in Alabama in 1956, Birmingham's activists created the Alabama Christian Movement for Human Rights and elected Reverend Fred L. Shuttlesworth as its President. When the group tried to desegregate buses, extremists bombed Reverend Shuttlesworth's home. The Reverend persuaded Dr. Martin Luther King, Jr. to make Birmingham the place for the next civil rights campaign.

The infamous legacy of Birmingham in the 50s and 60s has been well documented, captured for prosperity in movies and documentaries. There were scenes of vicious dogs latched to the hands of helmeted and armed cops leading an attack against Civil Rights marchers under the leadership of the prince of racism, Bull Conner, the chief of police. What wasn't depicted was the forging of Black women, men and children—a culture robbed of humanity—into a tight-knit protectorate sense of community. In many ways typical, we represented a microcosmic Black community of American Africanism, having always had to think outside the White American box because of our African ancestry and our experiences and the continual brutal reaction to us by the larger population. We had evolved into a people determined to survive, succeed, and achieve. Not all days were rife with one controversy or another, but there were few idyllic, lazy southern days for us. Something was always going on. Maybe that explained why the Black community simply referred to the city as the "Ham" because it was always showing off.

A racial caste system existed that either kept Blacks out, or kept them in low-paying jobs. In many respects, this system—formerly referred to as Jim Crow—still exists, having been in existence long before Emancipation, documented in the US census as far back as 1790. (The categories used during slavery were never really abandoned.) Looked upon as a demographic marker by many, the census was and remains demonstratively an instrument of power, as during its inception was used to advance race science (Nobles, 2000). Utilizing the same categories (Black, White, and mulatto) on the census reinforced social race (folk beliefs about human variation), which legitimized race and allowed it to be used as a criteria in employment. However, by using the classic anthropological concept of race, researchers' never defined race, and the criteria for assignment to a racial category was never stated (Cooper and David 1986; Jones et. al, 1991). In using race, the federal government collaborated with race science to make races real—a definite display of power. They saw no need to change it even after Emancipation. I should add that the census today is like the brass ring as it is jostled by different political (and racial) persuasions vying for the gifts its numbers bestow.

Nevertheless, Blacks in Birmingham were often used as strikebreakers in what was called a split-labor market, meaning that for the same job, skill and education, Blacks were paid less than Whites. This contributed to making race more important than class, and is part of the reason why Blacks and Whites never got together against the upper class; even though, such a coalition was not without precedent.

White Alabamians seemed well informed about Bacon's Rebellion where in 1676, Black servants and poor Whites joined together to rebel against the ruling class in Virginia (Smedley, 1999). This coalition could not be allowed, and as punishment, rights were withdrawn from Blacks and Native Americans, while more rights and privileges were bestowed upon poor Whites; thus creating a class aristocracy, with Blacks at the bottom with no rights, while poor Whites were in the middle and upper class Whites were at the top of the milieu. Of course, all Whites were potential aristocrats.

After slavery, Whites got to work in the mills, but Blacks were kept on the plantation because they had debt. Albeit incredible, due to the debt-peonage system, Blacks (recently freed African Americans) couldn't leave the plantation without paying off their debt. America reneged on her promise of 40 acres and a mule to these recently freed men and women. For if they didn't pay for their room and board after Emancipation, they were recaptured and returned as convicts! Instead of real Emancipation, they went from slavery to neoslavery (a legal system of slavery). We were free, but only as second-class citizens.

This epitomized the history looming over my head as the daughter of Alice and James Hutchinson. Next to the youngest, I have two older siblings, Edward and Brenda and a younger brother, Kerry. We nicknamed him Mooshe after a mischievous little boy who used to be in a Walt Disney movie.

I think I'm an anthropologist today because of my family. My father used to take me to museums; it was one of my favorite forms of entertainment. When we traveled north to visit his sisters, we always stopped at historical landmarks, which were met with delight, as well, for it fueled my curiosity and quenched my thirst to learn.

My parents always promoted education as the key to a good life, a way out from under the oppressive claws of White domination. Possessing a character trait seemingly inherent in most Black parents, they wanted more for me than they had for themselves.

When I was about nine my mother bought a set of *World Book Encyclopedias*. I read about the Masai, the elegant, dark-skinned people of Kenya and custodians of their beloved cattle, and the Great Wall in China. Awed by the majesty captured in the pictures, I wanted to go to those places. But until that time came, I thought I could get all the knowledge I would ever need just by reading the encyclopedias. And starting with "A", I read all of them; yet, my subconscious lingered on the first one, where I discovered anthropology and archaeology.

Meanwhile, I was contented where we lived—113 Eleventh Avenue North. My parents were the working poor. My father was a nurse's aid at the Veteran's Hospital and my mother was a cook. She often had two to three jobs. Mama worked during the day and daddy always had the nightshift.

Sometimes my mother would wake me at three in the morning, disturbing my sleep, so she could comb my hair before she went to work. After that I would have to sleep a certain way so I wouldn't mess it up. At other times my father combed my hair before I went to school, which was a more favorable arrangement. He was also quite adept at cooking, sewing, grocery shopping, ironing, and doing a slew of other domestic chores since he was at home during the day. For a long time I thought all men did that. What a disappointment!

My father used to ride a bicycle although he had a car. Working at the V.A. hospital, he believed in staying in good physical condition. He often walked around Legion Field and rode his bike to town. It was kind of embarrassing at the time because my friends would call and say things like, "I saw your dad on a bike. What's wrong with him? Why doesn't he drive his car?" At seventy-two years old, he was still walking. While we never knew why, we tried to stop him from walking the sixteen-mile round trip to town and back, but he would leave the house before my sister could pick him up. Everyone in the neighborhood knew his habit and offered him a ride. Most of the time he refused a ride.

We had a large backyard, the stage of many childhood dramas. There were fig and pecan trees in the backyard, but mostly, kids came to play baseball. We also had a plastic swimming pool that my sister nearly drowned my brother in: she wanted to see how long he could hold his breath. Most of the time, we dressed in costumes and pretended to be super heroes. One night, my friend Drake, replete in his Spider Man costume, jumped off the roof. He landed on the back porch and sprained his leg in the process. When confined inside, either by dark or the weather, we entertained ourselves with all sorts of childish and sometimes, foolish antics. Once, we took a fishing reel with plastic bats hooked on the end and hung it in front of my mother who was lying on the sofa. She screamed, but eventually laughed about it. (We sweated bullets in the time it took for her to find the humor in our playfulness.)

But being outside was always more fun. We used to sit on the back porch, telling each other ghost stories. Whenever my Aunt visited, she scared the bee-Jesus out of us with her frightening tales. She always gave us a quarter before she left. That was enough for a couple of candy bars and some bubble gum! Those times left fond memories, like Birmingham at sunset when wonderful illusions took possession of the nightmares of the day.

We lived in Smithfield. Smithfield was (and remains) an all Black neighborhood with middle and low-income families. It represented "community" in the traditional sense of the word, an exalted ideal of beneficial relationships in a certain geographical area, clustered around an ideology of what it meant to be Black.

About eight miles south of White downtown, Smithfield connected to our downtown. Unless one had business or worked there, there was no reason to go into the White world. Everything was segregated anyway. Why go downtown to the department store, spend dollars to sit at the lunch counter, only to end up in jail? A certainty, jailing resulted as well if one got on an elevator marked "White Only." These were risks not worth taking, as we didn't have to leave the neighborhood to purchase anything we needed, or wanted.

Fourth Avenue housed the Black downtown, completely furnished with the Masonic temple and other Black owned businesses—shoe shops, eating establishments, and two theatres, the Carver and Famous. They were proudly ours, and they received our hardy support. We also owned beauty salons, a fancy restaurant, Sugar Hill, and of course, Mr. Golston's corner store where we bought our candy.

Most of the movies that came to the Carver or Famous had already been shown at the White theatres. We saw advertisements for movies on television long before we could actually see the movies at our village theatres. When 'Cinderella" played at the Alabama, a White theatre, I wondered why they showed the advertisement for that movie on television when I couldn't go there to see it? And if I couldn't go, why did I even need to know about it? I felt it was manipulation on their part, a way to psychologically destroy by telling us these things existed, knowing we would be denied experiencing them. "Nah-Nah-Nah-Nah-Nah-Nah."

As it turned out, the movie was all right, but not nearly as great as the hype.

Now when the film *Superfly* came out, the entire community was abuzz with excitement to see it. No one in our community dressed "cool" and "slick" with hair permed straight like the Ron Ely character. A *Superfly* in Birmingham risked torture and arrest by the police. Still, while we couldn't identify with the movie, we longed to see someone who looked like us on the big screen, and that alone was gratifying.

Unlike today where drug dealers hang out on street corners, openly selling drugs to anyone passing by, the dealers during my days stayed in their homes. We knew where the drug dealers resided; you just didn't go there. And if people wanted drugs—heroin was the big addiction attraction—they went inside to purchase them, then returned to their cars and left. But I don't think the community would have tolerated them if they hadn't been low key about their operation. Openly selling drugs on the streets was simply not allowed; for one, it was too disrespectful. The dealers left the community alone, in a way, and the community left them alone. I often wished *they* had left us alone, too.

David J. Vann, the mayor of Birmingham in the seventies, put vest pocket parks in Black communities. Before that time city improvements in Black communities were almost unheard of, consequently it became a memorable phenomena. Our communities were allowed to erode into disrepair and stayed that way because Black people didn't have money for upkeep and maintenance, and the city didn't invest in them. These parks were an important gesture to the Black community in that while they weren't much—a swing, slide, basketball court and benches on a corner lot—they were better than the nothing we had before.

Housing projects were also located in the community, but class distinctions did not exist. While some Blacks had more than others, at gas stations we all had to walk around the back to use the "Colored Only" restrooms. We all drank from the "Colored Only" water fountains and we all ate in the basement at Woolworth.

We had to move to Cottage Hill, a middle-class neighborhood, because the city built a freeway through our community. They built it through our community because they didn't want to destroy a Jewish cemetery where people were already dead. Instead, they got the living Black people to move to a new village. Black people neither then nor now possessed the clout at city hall to prevent it.

My father moved our house from Smithfield to Cottage Hill, but again, we were the poorest people there. I think my father decided that since he didn't have money, he would put us in nice surroundings, which is what he did. At the time it was a hassle because who wants to be in the most poverty stricken looking house in the neighborhood? But it was and has continued to be a nice neighborhood, and I'm eternally grateful that my father had the insight to move us there.

So we were in a middle-class neighborhood with Black families who owned newspapers; Angela Davis' family lives there. In fact, there was a lot of economic variation in the community as lower-income and middle-income Blacks lived in the same community. The steel mills were central to the economy of Birmingham and also to the United States, especially during WWII. They employed a lot of Black people with less than a high school education. They made good money, working in Sippecoe, the nearby industrial area of town. Men and women had more self-esteem because they were working and women knew where men were during the day. Still, we were all Black, our common bond and the reason we lived together. Occupation didn't matter either. Neither job nor money could buy you out of racism.

This was a time of communal living. Cottage Hill was a village, following the proscription of the African proverb: "It takes a whole village to raise a child." Within our village were intricate social networks that made survival possible. For example, we could eat breakfast at anyone's house and it wasn't a big deal because we were all family. And all the adults were your parents and they could punish you. (We better not had cried child abuse!) People whose window you broke while playing ball, or whose porch you dirtied while playing with mud pies were your parents; they dealt with you as if you were their own child. And then you had to deal with Mama and Daddy, as the grapevine was alive and well: you could bank on your parents knowing what you'd been up to by the time you got home.

One time while walking to the store, I walked in the middle of the street because I didn't want to continually say, "good evening, good evening, good evening." Since everyone sat on his or her front porch I would have to 'speak.' By the time I got home my mother knew I hadn't spoken to Mrs. So-and-so. Boy, did she give me a good tongue lashing for not saying good evening to her! On a different occasion I grabbed a hand full of cement from one of my neighbor's new walkway. The woman saw me, came outside and gave me a spanking. When I got home, my mother knew what had happened, and I got another spanking. Eyes were everywhere!

Here the vegetable man came in a wagon led by horses each morning. Everyone bought fresh vegetables. We had a milkman, fresh and delivered daily. I used to run up the street and ride back down to my house on the milkman's truck. It goes without saying that we knew the milkman, the vegetable man, and the postman. In fact, we knew pretty much everybody that came into the area. We knew them by name and they knew our names.

There were also informal exchanges. For example, Mrs. Stokes, who lived across the street, made my dresses. My mother starched the hell out of our dresses. She soaked them in starch and hung them on the clothesline outdoors. After she ironed them, they stood up with a stiff military bearing like someone was already in them. I had to keep my arms stretched out from my side so the crispness of the dress wouldn't cut me.

People knew where you were all the time. There were always older-retired people in the neighborhood. Some people worked in the steel mills at night so they were at home during the day. If I was outside playing there were eyes watching me. Somewhere somebody was watching, someone knew where I was and someone knew what I was doing and whom I was with. So, in that sense, also, it was a very safe environment because you were always taken care of. I guess you could say there was communal daycare because the village was the daycare center.

Even if your mother wasn't looking out the window at you every moment (although it seemed like she was), someone was looking out the window and someone knew what you were up to. A person could not come into the neighborhood, pick up a child and disappear. People would at least know the car and maybe who picked the child up. There was a feeling of community that converted into a sense of security.

In my childhood there were no White people in the community. Whites lived in the area once, but when Blacks moved in they fled; some Jews stayed however. (Typically, their children still own homes in the neighborhood today.) Nevertheless, White people did not come into Black communities unless they had some type of business there, such as the police (cause for immediate alarm), insurance salesmen, people selling encyclopedias, or something like that. Otherwise, they didn't go into Black homes. Ditto for us: we went to White neighborhoods only to work. The White neighborhood was a dangerous place. You could be harassed there. This is the type of information we got from adults.

The two neighborhoods, Smithfield and Cottage Hill, were contiguous. Cottage Hill was on a hill and maybe it had a few more middle-class Blacks, but it never felt different in terms of village life.

Life has changed, however. The sense of community identification that we once shared has been lost to us. In a nutshell, integration downsized our community. Now we can go to stores where they treated us disrespectfully before. We no longer have to eat in the basement. With integration we have lost not only Black-owned businesses, but also the cohesion that was generated by segregation that existed as a common enemy. By moving into integrated neighborhoods, we forfeited what little political clout we possessed, for it remains to be seen if Black candidates can be elected without drawing lines, making more boxes.

Integration was inevitable and necessary, but it benefited Whites more than Blacks. In addition to bringing about a loss of the communal way of life we enjoyed, we also couldn't forget what we didn't have before it, and people very much wanted to forget the past indignities. They wanted to be equal, even if equality didn't (doesn't) exist. With integration, we lost the bond of fighting for equality, replaced by an individual effort. People now view equality in economic terms, not just social terms. Now, we have class differences where the concept of "Black community" seems like a misnomer. There is no more Mrs. Stokes to sew our dresses, no Mrs. So-And-So to avoid on the way home, no one to watch out for the children.

No more WE.

Chapter Two

Promise in the Air

"Today I will not capitalize america in my paper until I'm ready to send it in for publication. It seems to make me feel good."

Bomb scares were commonplace: we had at least one everyday in elementary school. Despite the humdrum of their potential, we took them seriously. A lot of people failed to realize that although it may not have been your home that was bombed, you still felt the repercussions of it. I have never been able to forget one occasion when a home in the neighborhood was bombed. Our house shook from the explosion and our windows shattered right along with our nerves. During those days, rage and fear became woven into the fabric of my existence. I worried about who was hurt, who was killed, who was not going to be around anymore? And it wasn't a question of whether it would happen again, but when?

Children worried. We worried about the adults. We worried about our friends going to school, about being in school, returning home, all the while anxious of what we would find when we arrived. Bomb threats made us fearful, so we walked to school in groups for protection, a salve for our mental and emotional security than anything else.

I went to Wilkerson Elementary School. This was a new school, located in the valley surrounded by homes. One of my teachers, Mrs. Crowell, suffered the experience of having her home bombed. The experience was replete with her son's injury as he came to school with his arm in a sling. Her husband had a business, and that was the connection, the justification for bombing their home.

They not only bombed the homes of people directly or actively involved in the Movement, but the homes of people who owned businesses, as well. I have speculated it was because they feared that the business owners funded the activists, if *they* weren't directly involved. So it appeared that not only did *they* not want us to have civil rights, *they* didn't want us to have economic power, either. *They* wanted us solely and totally dependent upon them. It was quite ironic: why depend upon someone when you knew they would deny you in the first place? Maybe the lesson was even simpler than that: we could have nothing *they* didn't want us to have, and *they* would ensure we would get nothing. They underestimated our mindset.

Nevertheless, the first through the fourth grades were fun because field trips were plentiful. They provided an opportunity for a brief respite from the harsh realities affecting our childhood, distracting our daily anxieties. We went to the symphony, the zoo, and the space center in Huntsville. All of those were uneventful, compared to my experience at Moundville National Park, when we went on a field trip when I was about in the sixth grade.

Moundville had one of the largest populations in North America, home to a sizeable population of American Indians who lived there from around A.D. 1000 to A.D. 1350. We called them Mississippian Indians (in Alabama, there were groups like the Choctaw and Cree). Of the twenty-six earthen mounds uncovered, one was incredibly huge; it was where the priests lived. The larger the mound, the higher your status, while the average person lived around the mound area. (The Moundville Archeological Park is viewable on line at http://museums.ua.edu/moundville). There were even small mounds in people's back yards in this area. I saw one where a fence ran over it, dividing the properties of two households.

The budding anthropologist in me thought it was the greatest thing that people lived on mounds. As we toured the museum I realized they built huts on top of the mounds to live in. Undoubtedly it was an important experience, helping to develop my interest in bones (osteology) because they left some burials in tact in the museum. I remember thinking that this person was buried here thousands of years ago and now we're looking at the body. There were a number of skeletons and some of them had grave goods, like pots, arrowheads, and beads. This was all fascinating to me!

Unfortunately, I ended the trip by making my close friends real upset with me. I thought I was helping them by filling their thermos with water. It was water from the outside and not the inside drinking water. I didn't know it but it smelled like "do-do." They thought I did it on purpose, but I really didn't. I swear!

Another of my most exciting days in elementary school came when the teacher introduced us to Neanderthals. She said they were people that lived thousands of years ago. My eyes lit up with awe and wonder. She said some people believed that human beings evolved from lower forms of life and not from Adam and Eve. Most people didn't believe that, however. I was just curious, so I went to my beloved encyclopedias to read about Neanderthals. In reading about their time on earth, I saw where my teacher failed to mention that they hunted, buried their dead and lived in caves where they used fire. In hindsight, I'm pretty sure she would have gotten into trouble if she did. She didn't discuss how evolution worked.

Things began to change around the seventh or eighth grade, for it was the height of the Civil Rights Movement. Sixteenth Street Baptist Church was a hotbed of activity, serving, as the headquarters where the demonstrations were planned, while Kelly Ingram Park, across the street, served as the starting point for the marches to downtown.

Since the one-story school building was in a valley, there were lots of windows. We could see our parents circling the building at the top of the hill. Fire trucks and police were on hand, as well, providing little more than a show of protection. Being on the main level may have lessened our curiosity, even though our anxiety wasn't abated when we took classes in the basement where we were even more vulnerable. Wondering what was going on above us, yet realizing the potential of the top floor collapsing in on us.

This untenable tensed situation was like a merry-go-round. Students were inside trying to adjust while our parents maintained a Monday through Friday vigilance, walking around the building, watching, and waiting, from the start of the school day until its end. They were sort of like vultures, too. It was hard to ignore their fear, which fueled our own. We were always ready to escape.

I can't tell you how utterly difficult it was during this time because all day long something was going on, and we knew what was going on. Still, we tried to follow our regular routine and deal with the likelihood of a bomb exploding at any time.

If the bell rang repeatedly, you simply left the building, and life went on. It was a normal abnormal way of living. It was like being in prison, constantly under siege, for we knew at any moment something terrible could happen. Yet, there was nothing we could do about it.

At the same time, it was expected that we would go on with classes. I don't really know how they expected us to concentrate on learning with everyone on edge all the time. People were suspicious of bags left in the hall. Garbage cans, receptacles where explosive devices could easily be hidden fell under guarded watch, at all times.

Concentration wavered on subject matter; it was hard to maintain focus on courses like English. At this point I was even questioning why we were learning English . . . when you consider the fact that White people didn't want us in this country. English was for Englishmen! I questioned our presence in this country: why stay where we weren't wanted? In typical adolescent rationale, it didn't make sense, for even though our parents had the right to vote and were citizens, none of us were accepted as American citizens. We could participate, but not fully. We couldn't go to any public facility. Signs over water fountains and bathroom doors directed us to where we could not go and where we had to go. So why learn the Englishman's language?

To this day, I have refused to capitalize America or any of its derivatives that begin with an "A" in my papers until I'm ready to send it in for publication. It seems to make me feel good.

Because of the tense situation during this precarious time, when our lives were as sacrosanct as cockroaches, we really didn't have to go to school at my house. My parents knew it was dangerous. But it was an option neither I nor my brothers and sisters wanted. We liked going to school. People in the neighborhood went to school or work because there really were no options. What were you supposed to do ... stay at home and be under siege? We were already on the front lines of the battlefield; staying home was not an option, but rather a siege mentality, and people refused to accept that closet lifestyle. Everyone lived as close to a daily life as was possible, either going to work or to school.

I never knew if there were really bombs when I attended Wilkerson. I doubted if anyone really knew. Of all those days that we left the building, they never told us. Still, we honored the fire drill ritual of walking in a single line and rushing outside, all the while fixated on conjecture, wondering whether this was the one when the school blew up? Would we get out in time? Who would plant a bomb in a school? Why would they kill us? I, like my peers, always knew the answer to the last question, however. White people would plant a bomb of destruction for no other reason than that we were Black.

Eating in the basement and drinking out of the color only water fountain represented the norm. It didn't mean we liked it, but our displeasure at the indignities wasn't limited to water fountain and restroom usage rules. And understand that it wasn't a big deal because we felt that White water fountains offered better or colder water, but rather because so much emphasis had been placed on something so simple and harmless. It was a symbol of asinine rejections based on nothing else but our skin color — their power, our helplessness, another slap in our faces.

One day we drove all day—at least, it seemed like it when I was around seven years old—to get to an amusement park. Once we arrived, the White guy very politely told us they did not allow Negroes in the amusement park. He apologized profusely for not allowing us in. In hindsight, he may have realized how silly the rule was, but he did nothing to change it. He was a nice racist. But neither did my father object. He exhibited no animosity of any sort, seemed to just take it in stride and didn't look bothered by it. It was like, "Okay, we can't get in, so we'll just turn around and go back home."

Since I suffered from carsickness, I was really upset about the whole day. To drive all day and then find out we can't go in because of our color! I was pissed-off!!

My dad probably expected it to happen. He probably prepared himself for it. Besides, he had experienced this all of his life. It was no surprise and if he made a fuss he could be arrested. What would be the point of that?

To some extent, you had to desensitize yourself while maintaining sensitivity. We couldn't let White racism throw us on the carpet by getting violent every time they exhibited some form of racial hatred. Martin Luther King's nonviolent approach was a perspective that Black people had already incorporated into their lives. He just institutionalized it in the Movement.

But damn, it sure was hard to abide, particularly when we knew another way of life existed elsewhere. We could tell when we crossed the Mason-Dixon Line.

Every summer we drove to Akron, Ohio and Milwaukee to visit my father's sisters. It was always great to get out of the south. The only problem was that we had to return. When we stopped at gas stations in the south, we had to use the colored only restrooms. We carried our own water because gas stations didn't usually have a separate water fountain for us.

Upon crossing the line, you could use any water fountain or restroom. When a friend of mine used to travel with her family, they carried a bucket because her mother didn't want them to use the restrooms. Still, looking at the situation of Blacks in the north, I didn't necessarily think they were better off. Racism was racism everywhere, north or south. While you could drink out of any water fountain, Blacks still couldn't get jobs that they were qualified for because of their heritage.

1967 was the first year of integration in Birmingham. Part of the promise that symbolized change, it received a hearty welcome. It was the dawn of a new adventure for me, and I intended to capitalize on it. Feeling that I already knew everybody who would be attending the neighborhood high school, Parker, I desired a different high school environment. Closing my eyes and pointing at a list of possible high schools, my finger landed on Ramsay, a predominantly White high school. Sharing my decision with friends turned out not to be prudent, for it was met with rejection, instead of acceptance. They taunted, accusing me of being a White girl. No amount of justification could allay their feelings that I was betraying Black people. Adding insult to injury, my light-skinned complexion didn't help. Instead of well wishes, my friends predicted my doom, not because I wasn't smart, but rather because "White people were smarter." They chided that I would make a fool out of myself.

In hindsight, they were possibly driven by fear. Not so much of physical violence, but of intellectual competition. There is little denying that European beliefs had a firm grip in the mindset of Blacks, as well as Whites. That Whites were smarter was not a new belief, not only among my friends at Wilkerson, but the community at large.

Anyway, Shirley refused to join me at Ramsay. She was my best friend, and while I wasn't ashamed of dark complexion, she was. So embarrassed by it she wouldn't even take school pictures because they were in Black and White, and made her look even darker. She was a beautiful girl, but because of her dark skin the mirror image she saw reflected "ugly". Eventually my friends got over my decision, but not until there had been an exchange of harsh words and ill feelings. Still, I had a lot to prove.

I never saw any reason for Whites to be smarter than Blacks, other than the fact that they had access to more books and exposure to more experiences. The weight of proving to my friends that they weren't smarter than us, however, posed a heavy burden, but a challenge relished nevertheless.

Considering everything that was going on, we (those of us bold enough to encroach on a White world) were immediately assailed with problems at Ramsay. Needless to say, there was a lot of suspicion between Blacks and Whites. Nobody understood, nor cared to try to get to know one another, at least initially.

My suspicions on one front, however, were well founded. Classes were liberally sprinkled with smart kids and dumb ones that varied among both Whites and Blacks. Going to Ramsay showed me that Whites were no different from Blacks in intelligence. But ignorance of one another made it easy to believe the stereotypes: the brain size of Whites allowed a greater potential to learn, while those of Blacks were smaller and proved the belief among Whites that Blacks were intellectually inferior.

There had been a couple of Blacks attending the school before massive integration. Prior to integration White schools might allow "two" Blacks to attend, in this case one male and one female. These students were there on a voluntary basis, although we were going there voluntarily, too. They had a different view of integration compared to us who were the new integratees. While we saw going to Ramsay as a liberation statement, part of the political struggle, the other two Blacks viewed our presence as an invasion of their school. Instead of being delighted that more Blacks attended school with them, they abhorred our presence.

Like all other aspects of society, Ramsay was a racist institution. Walking down the hall was a hassle because White students tried to bump you around. Whenever the bell rang and we had to change classes, walking through the hall was always a challenge, like maneuvering an obstacle course. We had to form defensive groups. Either we walked together, simply pushed and bulldogged our way through until we got to our locker or class, or we used Yvette. A big "football playing" looking girl, like an offensive lineman, she barreled down the hall and we followed in single file behind her as she pushed people out of the way so we could pass.

Of course, not all of the teachers were terrible or anything like that. Some teachers helped us sign petitions and worked on our behalf. One teacher stood with us and went to the principal to discuss our concerns. He was from the old South and would say things in class like "Negras and Negresses." Every time he said it, we all seemed to cringe.

Finally, one day in class we raised our hands and told him that the terms were inappropriate. We didn't like the use of the word Negra nor Negress and encouraged him to refer to us as "Black." He apologized and explained where he was brought up that was considered as being polite. Negra was considered a better word than nigger.

I remembered that incident because it raised an issue that on the surface appeared contradictory. How could he help us on one hand, then turn around and call us "Negresses" or "Negras"? It clarified the role of ignorance in the relationship between Blacks and Whites. Ignorance created animosity and contributed to the perpetuation of stereotypes. I also realized that while other people might want to support Blacks and our causes, their biases, upbringing, and history sometimes prevented them from accomplishing their goal, which was establishing friendship. Race was always an issue; therefore, racism was an issue and affected all relationships. (Ain't nothin changed.)

The cafeteria workers (all Black except the supervisor) at Ramsay were underpaid and overworked. They demonstrated because of poor working conditions, so we (the Black students) supported them by not eating in the lunchroom. This really distressed the principal and the cadre of White teachers and students.

At this point, Black students were about one third of the student body (my junior year). We voted in a block. White students ran different people for the same office. We would win with only one candidate. Eventually, they figured it out, but by that time we owned the victory.

By my senior year we were about equal in numbers, which somewhat leveled the playing field with regards to student activities, the field was warped by asinine rules constructed by the principal. In a way, he reconstructed the rules of the game, tantamount to the adage that 'every time we learn the rules, they change the game,' for whatever Black students liked to do, the principal made a rule against it. We had this courtyard area where during the lunch hour Black students would go and play their radios. Before we came along, White students apparently didn't go out onto the courtyard. We flocked out there, to escape the confines of being indoors and to listen to our music. The principal decided to make a rule against it. (Maybe he thought we were planning a resurrection.) That really unsettled the Black student body because there had been no rule against it before we came. And that's the way it went. Whatever we liked to do, they created a rule against it when a rule had never existed before.

We didn't acquiesce quietly. We knew how to organize a demonstration and did, to let them know that they couldn't get away with their power games. Even though it was usually for naught, demonstrating was the only way to voice our displeasure and get their attention.

High school was like that amusement park to which my family was denied entry. As they could not legally deny us the right to a public education anywhere we chose, they created other ways to impede us, throwing up obstacle after obstacle. But our coping skills were high. Taking from the example shown by my dad when he wordlessly accepted our rejection from the amusement park and took us away on our business, I went on about my business in high school by joining the band.

The band proved itself a healthy and successful outlet for me. We had a series of band directors, most of them White, some of them Black, and I remember one was a White woman named Mrs. Miller. She had a really hard time because people seemed to think that a woman shouldn't be a band director. Mrs. Miller awarded me the John Phillips Sousa Award for Outstanding Bandsmen, and it was quickly rumored that she got into trouble for that because they didn't feel it should go to a Black person. It had never happened before. She didn't return the following year. Actually, I think she didn't return because they didn't think a woman should be band director. It awakened my awareness to sexism. I never thought about sexism in the Black community before, although I knew on a subconscious level that it existed.

By my senior year, the band was equally divided between Black and White students. It was interesting in that we considered ourselves friends and interacted at school and even on band trips, et cetera, but we never visited each other's homes. There was nothing in real-life Birmingham even close to the TV drama series, "Any Day Now," about the special relationship between two women in a southern town, one Black, "Rene" (Lorraine Toussaint) and the other White, "Mary Elizabeth, M.E." (Annie Potts). Our school friendships never progressed to the point of going to each other's homes. It remained a mystery as to how this oddity was understood, other than the subject never came up in a discussion of any measure of friendship or anything else; it was just understood and accepted. Nor was it a problem, but rather part of the reality of the times and our lives. I didn't invite them to my house and they didn't invite me to theirs. And that was not only true for me personally, but other people as well. Yet, we were friends, sharing some kind of anonymous-friendship.

A Black high school, Hayes High, closed and students there were forced to attend Ramsay. They represented a different group of Blacks; I guess you might say, because they came against their will. Those of us already at Ramsay had come by choice. Although it created some new dynamics among the Black students, it didn't negatively affect the solidarity in terms of dealing with Whites. When it came time to run for elected offices, like for president of the student body and such, the Black students unified. In my junior and senior years, we pretty much ran the high school because of this solidarity.

We had one prom with a Black band. At the time it was cool to have a Black band play for the prom. This was the era of the hippie movement, so White students were all for it. However, tradition ruled at prom. We were separated, with Blacks dancing in one group and Whites in their group. During the prom the two groups sort of merged to some degree, with surprising results. We experienced group realization—Black and White students—that we were actually dancing together. We all froze in momentary shock. Then we separated, the Whites returning to their corner of the dance floor, and we to ours. It was a "No, No." You're not supposed to do that.

It's kind of funny now when I think about the look on some people's faces when they realized they were dancing together. Today, in 2005, still, there are Black and White proms. We didn't have that type of thing, but high school was nevertheless a "trip."

Chapter Three

Light, Bright, Damn Near ...

"Am I American or am I a Negro? Can I be both? Or is it my duty to cease to be a Negro as soon as possible and be an American?"
W.E.B. DuBois, 1897
American Negro Academy

Colorism is a pressing issue in the Black community as previously mentioned, and probably the bad root from which all other ills stemmed. It has existed in our community since slavery, and no doubt, because of it, for colorism is a system that classifies Blacks according to how closely our appearance resembles or conforms to the European standard of beauty. Even more quarrelsome is that it raises a challenging question of identity.

Living under the strains of oppression that has created a tradition of hurt caused us to reconfigure our culture, having been stolen from one and denied another. One result has been what W.E.B. DuBois in 1908 referred to as "double consciousness"—a dual window through which we were aware of self and simultaneously aware of others', namely Whites, perception of us. And within this schizophrenia or duality where we have forged two cultures—one African and the other American—to create a new one, American Africanism, resides colorism, a Freddie Kreuger in our midst. Dubois has been more than merely vindicated, predicting that the problem of the twentieth century was the problem of the color line, as the twenty-first century has arrived, and the color line remains a problem.

Even though quite a bit has been discussed and debated regarding slavery, especially with regards to reparations of late, enough can't be said about the residual effects of this horrendous American institution. Freed of physical bondage for more than a century, in many respects, we are still chained to slavery-old myths, stereotypes, beliefs and behaviors of a self-destructive quality. It has marred everything representative of African American culture as ugly, inferior, of little consequence, and /or outright, no good—until or unless appropriated, thus redefined or reconstructed and stamped "acceptable."

Nor fine art, food or music has escaped this branding, and certainly, not us who have shamefully embraced this insipid practice, devaluing those things uniquely ours, us, when we demean them and each other, thus diluting our strength and beauty by committing intra-racial discrimination. This expression of self-hatred, also known as the "color complex," colorism, has held reference not only to our skin tone, but to our hair, and the size and shape of our nose and lips, as well.

Ironically, it came to my personal attention innocently enough with a nickname. Naming, a function of rhetoric in all cultures, is a component of colorism because it revolves around or reverts back to identity. Names, like labels, stick, once pasted onto one's identity, and unpleasant names seal like superglue.

Based on African tradition, names represented a way to control one's life. To some degree African Americans retained the memory and practice of this African convention, taken largely from the Mandingo, Yoruba, and Ibo. Children were given two names on the continent. Babies were named for the day of the week, month or season of birth, birth order, or circumstances, such as head presentation of a lengthy pregnancy or a cord around the neck. Additionally, Africans stressed clan names, such as crocodile, or other animals and plants. *Ali*, for example, was a name given to the fifth male child born in the Mandingo. In the Congo, *Lonzo* meant inordinate sexual desire, while in Yoruba, *Ayoka* was one who caused joy (*The Gullah People and their African Heritage* by William S. Pollitzer, 1999).

Consequently, English nicknames abided with African practice that dealt with appearance, relationship, or personality. For instance, *Blue* was a nickname given to people with very dark skin color. *Prosper* was given to someone predicted to become successful in the community. *Bubba* was the equivalent of "brother" in English, and *Betsy Ben* indicated that Ben was the son of Betsy (Pollitzer, 1999).

Since we subscribed to this African-based practice of giving one another nicknames, skin tone was often used to describe people. They were called "Yellow", "Red", "Black", "Brownie", "Redbone, et cetera, depending on complexion. I was "Fox" in elementary school, and later "Red' in high school, while in college they called me "Hutch." Today, I sometimes go by my African name, Yaa, a female child born on Thursday.

Calling each other out of our names, then, was a seemingly harmless, playful indulgence ... until. Whenever my brother was angry with me, he called me "White Girl," knowing full well it would hurt my feelings. It just wasn't that my feelings were hurt. Hurt feelings were commonplace, as this widespread, albeit innocent custom created fission in the community.

People have always been fascinated by skin color, and I was no different. As in many families, the skin tones in mine ranged from the extremely dark to the extremely light. This was the prelude to my keen interest over color as a child.

Although not with revulsion or suspicion, I wondered how the variation happened in my family. (I didn't know about the tricks and talents of genetics then.)

My curiosity went beyond the visible self, as I also wanted to know why it was so painful when challenged or teased about my complexion. Name-calling seemed akin to playing the "Dozens," designed to be hurtful, but not to be taken seriously. Being called a White girl, however, hurt. Neither could I forget my childhood friend who wouldn't allow her lovely, baby-soft dark face to be captured in Black-and-White photos. Light-skinned or dark skinned, we were all treated the same. I mulled my disconcerted curiosity for a long time, but I don't think I ever got over the hurt; even though I know more now than I did then.

The Webster Dictionary of the 16th century defined black as dirty, evil, and darkness, while pure, clean, good, and virginal on the other hand, were associated with white. The biology of Africans, our dark skin in particular, was seen as an indicator of our sub-humanness and closeness to lower forms of animals. Hence, we were at the bottom of the human evolutionary tree, perceived with enmity as subhuman. Black women especially bore the brunt of this brutality, incapable of ever living up to the standards of beauty. Except in the ownership of the doll we craved, there would be "No synthetic yellow bangs suspended over marble-blue eyes, no pinched nose and bowline mouth" (*The Bluest Eye*, Toni Morrison, 1994: 1920) for us. Yet, this model was deeply embedded in our collective subconscious as the beauty of which to aspire, to desire, and to treasure. Black men desired this product, and Black women aspired to become this product.

It's interesting, yet painfully condescending, as well, how Black people treat you differently if you were dark or light-skinned. "*If you get yourself a Black man, he'll love you to death,*" My mother always told me. This persistent belief held, and still does among many of us, that a dark-skinned man would somehow love a light-skinned woman better than if she were of a dark complexion. I believe the conclusion, as well as the origins are obvious, stemming from slavery, from having always had the model of beauty paraded before him, and for a long time the closest replica was a light skinned woman.

As if being Black wasn't enough, dark skin branded one with the permanent and inescapable label of "ex slave"—unlovable, unacceptable, incapable of humanity. "A dark woman can't do anything for me", says Bill who himself is light complected (Michel Marriott, 1991 (November):118, Essence).

It has been assumed that light-skinned people have been more educated, thus wealthy — as if one equated the other — than those with darker complexions. Of course and again, the idea originated in slavery, where the slave master singled out, bred with and/or raped an enslaved African female to produce an individual that bore his traits, believing the result was someone more intelligent, more responsible, in other words, better than a 'pure' Black person. This gave birth to negative terms such as "field nigger" and "house nigger," whereby the latter received less stringent work along with the semblance of benefits. The former, figuratively and literally, slaved in the fields. However, mulattos (usually house servants) were never considered "mixed Whites" (Nobles, 2000).

While they were never considered "mixed Whites" by anyone but us, we saw the surface blessings bestowed upon them as replicas of, if not the ideal standard of beauty with their "good hair", 'bright skin" and 'delicate facial features." The offspring of enslaved mothers fathered by the master were often educated. Such relationships could result in freedom for the mother and her child, and they might also receive an inheritance, thus resultant in their education and/or financially secured position in society. The descendants of such unions often became leaders in the Black community, blessed in our eyes with wealth and education, models to both envy and aspire.

Whites behaved, as did many Blacks when it came to skin tone among Blacks. This was seen, for example, when a White professor incessantly called on lighter-skinned Blacks in class. It was incorrectly assumed that the professor was acknowledging your intelligence or somehow elevating you. You were still "beneath" them in their eyes. But because you were light skinned, you were considered *less Black*. Being less Black meant that you didn't conform to all of the racist stereotypes. Because of your close physical representation that revealed the strain of White blood in your features, a chance existed for your educability. A shade of brightness moved you a notch up the evolutionary tree. Such a practice was duplicated, particularly after Civil Rights legislation became enforceable—although most likely originated in the workforce—whereby a lighter skinned African American was most likely hired over one, promoted, and perceived as most likely to fit in with the company than one with darker skin. It was euphemistically called the "mulatto hypothesis" (Russell et. al, 1992). Equality seemed skewered as some of us, the lighter skinned ones, were elevated and treated with a semblance of societal acceptance, while the darker faced received scorn and rejection based on skin color.

However, they who controlled the job market and education, were the yardstick against which we measured ourselves, and in the process, we lost sight of our history. The physical manifestation of our identity evolved into a near obsession whereby we mocked and deliberately hurt each others' feelings because of the colors of our skin. This, even as we struggled for the right to be self-determinant, to define ourselves by refusing to be categorized by others, we classified ourselves on a complexion scale, believing we'd achieved some monumental sense of self.

It was why when the Black Power Movement arrived in the sixties, it held lots of promise toward eradicating the complexities of colorism, coming replete with a campaign slogan designed to improve our image of our Black skin. "I'm Black and I'm Proud" was the battle cry of this emotional revolution. We sang it; we danced to it, styled our hair into Afros and dressed in Dashikis in exclamatory celebration that "Black is Beautiful." We rejoiced, at last, having something to shout about in being Black.

It was great while it lasted; however, there was a down side. While the skin color phenomenon initially involved the rejection of darker-skinned African Americans by their lighter brethren, the table reversed with dark-skinned African Americans sometimes spurning their lighter-skinned brothers and sisters for not being Black enough during the Black Power period, reverse self-discrimination. Still, this walk tall sense of pride didn't completely penetrate the group mindset nor did it perpetuate generationally. For once the Black Power Movement waned and doors of opportunity opened, the complexities surrounding color continued.

Clinging vehemently onto a slave master's "darkie" image of us, we have been embroiled in this ridiculous fight over who's Black and who's not, maybe even still unconscious of the damage we do ourselves. Nevertheless, I have seen it retard the efforts of community-based organizations in a membership divided by this colonial-based method of divide-and-conquer. Challenges of who was qualified to lead, or whose idea was valuable enough to adopt were launched simply because the one who made a suggestion was either dark or light-skinned, had permed hair or dreadlocks, wore African attire or American clothes.

In *Genealogical Shifts in DuBois's Discourse on Double Consciousness as the Sign of African American Difference* Bernard Bell and Emily Grosholz (1996) wrote, "Contemporary global ethnic conflicts also suggest that the correlative problem or sign of double consciousness will be central to identity formations in the twenty-first century"(Bell et al., 1996: 88). The enmity that results in identity conflicts have been lethal, as was evidenced in the conflicts between the Serbs and Croatians and the Tutsi and Hutus in the name of cultural cleansing. With such precedents, we dare not exclude the probability of similar incidents on our own land.

I have come to believe that the reason we continue this farce of "Blackness" is because we don't know what it means. Combined with the possibility that our self-hatred is skin deep. Nevertheless, we seemed blinded by the fog of racism's new subtle hue, tricked into believing that we are indeed "free at last." While we liken it to skin color or ancestry, Blackness is a way of life that includes not only our skin color, but speaks to our commitment to freedom and equality, our consciousness of what those aspirations mean for our collective achievement and advancement. Again, in the words of DuBois, "...Have we in America a distinct mission as a race, a distinct sphere of action and an opportunity for race development, or is self-obligation the highest end to which Negro blood dare aspire? ..." (Bell et al., 1996: 90).

Am I Black Enough for You?

Chapter Four

Plantation Work Ethics

"The best food was in the basement anyway."

In the capitalist society in which we live, man hasn't a chance of being anything other than a slave without money and education: that appeared to have been what 'the man" had in mind for us. Emancipation raised a number of issues for America that revolved around what to do with its mass of newly freed enslaved Africans. After all, they needed a place to live, a way to feed themselves, some mechanism by which to survive. Unanswered, these issues explained why many predicted the extinction of the African on American soil; otherwise, this new crop of African American would have to join the workforce by competing for jobs traditionally assigned as *belonging* to Whites. This could not be allowed!

The push for civil rights did not begin with desegregation in Brown v. Board of Education or Rosa Parks refusal to sit in the back of the bus in Montgomery, Alabama. It began with attempts to dismantle southern segregation (D'Angelo, 1999). In existence already was the 1875 Civil Rights Act, which guaranteed Blacks equal rights. But the mind set of racism was cemented and hardened in place that not even freed Blacks were equal to Whites, and the north had already created a model that governed the separation of the races. It was called Jim Crow. Through manipulation of institutions, intimidation, and violence, Blacks in the south were subjugated and White power was restored. This system of segregation began in 1877 after the end of the Reconstruction period in which a racial caste system was created in the American south (D'Angelo, 1999). Some historians demarcate the 1890s through 1954 as the era of segregation, although it lingered through 1969 (Loewen, 1999).

After reconstruction was complete and the Union soldiers gone, the south faced problems regarding the transition from slavery to freedom on a larger scale than the north. Realizing the dilemma created by this new workforce that also lacked the ability to compete, as an education had been prohibited and even illegal during slavery, *America offered as a start-up "40 acres and a mule."*

Still, it was insufficient to fill the void of this social and economic predicament. Since they never got the land or animals this point was mute.

Consequently, the south borrowed from their northern brethren who had already deconstructed the 1875 Civil Rights, implementing Jim Crow as a legalized caste system, which effectively prevented competition between Whites and Blacks on all levels. It landed an especially hard blow to our economic welfare. Especially since America reneged on her promise of 40 acres and a mule, as well.

Jim Crow, the title of a demeaning minstrel song that became associated with Blacks, was the south's response to a free economy for Blacks (Quite similar to when one hears the term, Affirmative Action; people automatically think of African Americans.) These laws contained some of the most insane and disgusting rules imaginable, such as, a colored person could not be buried on the same ground of a White person, convicts should be separated along racial lines, Blacks and Whites could not play dominoes or checkers together, to name a few. Nevertheless, Jim Crow served its purpose of severely affecting our ability to earn a decent living.

In Birmingham's White downtown, Black people could work upstairs, but not eat upstairs: we had to eat in the basement. You may have wondered why not walk a few blocks to the Black downtown to eat, the answer seemed simple enough to us: when things have always been a certain way, the abnormal becomes the normal and people simply go on with life.

Aside from at home, the best food was in the basement anyway, in places like Woolworth. I think this was deliberate and a way for Black people to get revenge since they were the cooks both upstairs and downstairs. Even when I worked at some hotels and cafeterias, the best food remained in the kitchen where we made our food separate from what we served on "the line." The food on the line was "White folks food." If you dropped something on the floor or if the food got dirt or a roach on it, you just put it back on the plate. It was a covert war where Whites were the enemy. They didn't realize it, but the enemy was cooking their food and serving it to them. Who knew what was in the food? People put all kinds of things in it, even urine.

I started working around fourteen years old at cafeterias and restaurants in Birmingham. At one hotel I worked on the line serving food. People going to the medical center often came there for lunch and dinner. Some people had open-heart surgery. So they would come in with their shirt open and a long wound where the surgery took place. It looked terrible, but we were told not to stare. That was hard. You had to look and the customers seemed to understand. Anybody would look at an incision that was somewhat open. I guess they had to let it heal in layers. You could see their flesh.

We were never paid on time and sometimes we weren't paid at all. Cooks, waiters, waitresses, dishwashers and busboys felt they owned part of the restaurant since they hadn't been paid. People would not steal. They saw it as what was owed to them since they were never paid their full wages. The owner would always be upstairs in the hotel. One of my jobs was to let him know when his wife was in the building. I would go up knock on the door and tell him his wife was in the cafeteria. He was usually either with another woman (he had a lot of women) or gambling. I always suspected that the mafia owned that hotel. At least that's what everyone said. He gambled away our wages and everyone knew it, but they weren't really pissed off with him. It was more like well he's done it again. People would take it as long as they could because jobs were hard to find. But there would come a time when they would have to get another job because they had to pay their bills. At the same time how can you look for another job when you have to be at work? People were kind of caught and hoped they would get their back wages.

My mother was the cook so everyone bowed to her. They not only wanted to eat, but they relished her cooking. My mouth still waters remembering just the typical breakfast at my house: salmon croquettes, eggs, rice, biscuits and jelly. While greens and cornbread were stables at nearly every other meal, what my Mama could do with wieners and hamburger meat with spaghetti — indescribably delicious!

In addition to being a dedicated cook, and maybe because of that, the young waiters who smoked marijuana in the back never bothered my mother. She said they were better than the ones who drank because the drinkers tended to fight and shoot up the place. The pot smokers just wanted her to cook them something to eat.

I worked at other hotels where it was pretty much the same. They always said serve them a lot of liquor first and then they won't care what the food tastes like and they were right. By the time we served them cold steaks, they were too drunk to know or care. They just slurped it up and thanked us for doing such a good job. Some of those parties would get really wild. They would take off their clothes and I would imagine have group sex. We would leave and the servers would talk about how White people had no morals.

There was so much corruption in terms of White owners and managers stealing everything that wasn't nailed down, doing hard-core drugs like cocaine and heroin and using women like prostitutes, my mother told me to stay away from them. If they tried to approach me they would have to deal with my mother. They knew that so they left me alone. Other young women weren't so lucky. They needed the job to feed their children. White owners and managers manipulated them and basically turned them into prostitutes.

Thinking about what adults were dealing with, I was only a child and I was tired of the harassment, the discrimination, the racism, the alienation and not feeling like a full U.S. citizen. If I felt that as a child, imagine the impact of such gross injustice on adults, denied an opportunity to provide for their families.

People were pretty much fed up. The promise of equal work for equal pay so stipulated in the Civil Rights Act seemed to have had little impact on my family's finances. The eighty bucks a week I earned allowed me a personal freedom that was liberating in that I could buy the things I wanted and needed, but our family economic lifestyle didn't improve.

In essence, an impoverished lifestyle served to divert our attention from the head of the monster and onto one of its tentacles. Poor and hungry, desirous of self-respect before our families and communities, we stopped fighting for ideas like equality, and instead fought for materialistic gain. However, this was nothing as grandiose as mansions and twelve-car garages, but simple things, like a better place to live, safety, a decent meal, peace, a future for the children.

Once again, racism punctured holes in our dreams for an equal share of the American pie. While a few tiny slices were doled out, most of us got none, or so little as to equate to nothing. Out of frustration, I once told my father that I wanted to join the Panthers, and to this day, I remember the look of "are you crazy?" on his face. I guess at the time, again, he was trying to save my life. That's what Black parents did at that time. They tried to save the lives of their children. They were fighting for their rights because I know my father voted. He did various things with the city to try to get lights put up on street corners and to get streets paved and was successful in a few of them, such as getting street lights put up.

Basically, we were still fighting for equality, and everyone fought our battles in different ways. I guess my own protest was attending a predominately White school and in doing so saying that I am a citizen and I can go wherever I want.

Now things have changed a lot in Birmingham. Not only are people cooking the food, but eating it upstairs as well. So score a brownie point for integration; however, I still have a problem eating in hotels and restaurants.

The biggest point holder; however, has remained in the hands of racist ideology — policies and practices unsympathetic to our economic plight. For an entire decade after passage of Title VII of the Civil rights Act of 1965, designed to address fair employment opportunity for us, entire industries and whole job sectors have continued to exclude Blacks (Hill and Jones, *Race in America*). And when we are included, we often have had to endure some of the most disgusting and demeaning behaviors conceivable in the workplace.

For instance, over 2400 former and current Black employees who faced racial discrimination in pay, promotion and a hostile work environment sued Georgia Power in Atlanta, a Fortune 500 Company. They described use of the "N" word by supervisors and that for decades Hangman's nooses hung at all eight plants. Workers cited numerous examples of being passed over for promotions although they had seniority and skills commensurate with the position. One African American woman, who had worked there for twenty years, earned $4,000 less than a White woman that she trained who was doing the same job.

Another African American female who worked there for sixteen years was given the title of senior, but not the money that went along with it. A Black supervisor analyst earned $37,000, while a White female analyst, with the same rank made $67,000 and a project analyst, a rank below her position and White, earned $42,000. A study of wages at Georgia Power showed that Blacks formed the bottom of the pay scale and earned 20% less than Whites (Dateline NBC, August 21, 2001).

Even as I was convinced that an education promised the best alternative to living in poverty and ignorance, I'm hard-pressed to say that Jim Crow ever died in reality.

Chapter Five

Segregation on the Sabbath

"I was invited, but had to attend my own church. But for the Grace of God, I could have been one of those four girls."

There was nothing special about Sundays at my house, but they were special nevertheless, simply because we attended church. For generations since slavery, the Black church provided the only organized social institution that offered us full participation outside the family. There was nothing second-class about us in the Black workshop experience.

Sundays at church was our world, exclusive of Whites. We already knew their beliefs with regards to race and wanted no parts of it. Religion was no different than every other aspect of White culture denied us. Even after adopting the faith of the slave owners, Christianity that allegedly cleansed an evil soul and made one pure, enslaved Africans who converted to the Christian faith were not entitled to freedom. Settling the matter, the 1667 Virginia legislature ruled that, "the conferring of baptisme doth not alter the condition of the person as to his bondage or freedome" (Benjamin Quarles, 1969: 36, *The Negro in the Making of America*).

Instead of preaching from the bible that God created man, they preached God created each race separately, and since all Blacks were descendents of Ham, were therefore condemned to perpetual servitude (Rice, 1972). A popular belief among scientists in the eighteen hundreds was polygenesism. It is the doctrine that God created human races separately. Each race was considered a separate species. In essence, biblical texts were deconstructed biblical to justify this notion that completely repudiates the Book of Genesis.

Segregation was a blessing on Sundays in church where our minister preached a biblical interpretation best described as a Black liberation theology. It was nothing as fancy as the name implied, but Black politics, the Black preacher, and the Black church comprised an inseparable triumvirate. It was partly due to the relative privilege that the minister held in the community even during slavery. This made the transition into politics a natural one for the most influential figure. Lastly, but not least, it was the nature of Black preaching itself that in the hands of a charismatic leader allowed a ritual freedom of expression whereby the preacher could sermonize about everything from prostitution, drug abuse, and male-female relationships to the White power structure. Black preaching recognized the pain of being Black in a racist society, equaling the emotional equivalent of the term "Black Power", although the slogan was never uttered in the sermon.

We had a set routine—up around seven to eat breakfast and get dressed in our Sunday best (meaning, Black patent leather shoes, lacy, nylon socks, laced-rimmed hats, and frilly dresses for me) before we headed for church where we might stay all day. There was nothing wrong with that.

Spiritual expression has always been central to the Black community. Everyone grew up in the church. Many went to church or at least felt they should go. I attended church pretty much all day on Sunday, plus a couple of times during the week for choir rehearsal, youth usher board, or bible study. Going to church was more than merely participating in a religious event, even though it was as good for our emotional souls as our spiritual redemption. In essence, church provided a social occasion whereby we could actually relish in our humanity, unfettered by the humiliation we suffered during the weekdays.

There was a song we used to hum. It had no words, but I have remembered it with heartfelt fondness. So powerful and poignant, the humming had a melancholy melody that made me feel as if it must have been handed down since the time of slavery. It was my favorite song because it had no words. It blended like sacred harmony with the call-and-response oral tradition that was an inherent feature of the Black church. You hummed it, then a minister or deacon or maybe someone in the congregation would say something to the effect of, "Lord, bless these people here today," and then everyone would join in humming again. Everyone knew it, when to sing it, and anyone could initiate it, a deacon, minister, or someone from the audience. As if some divine cue fell from the rafters, everyone seemed to also know when to hum and how long the humming should last.

I don't remember the name of this song. It's not that I've forgotten it. I never knew it. I have never been sure whether it even had a name. It didn't need one, but it seemed to vanquish the deadly drone of racism witnessed and experienced during the week.

Come Sunday mornings, there were no "Negras, Negresses, or Niggers"; no "boys" or "gals/girls." Instead, our adults became Mr., Mrs., or Miss., titles, which they wore like crowns of glory, and children accorded them their due. More than Sunday etiquette where we learned no person on earth was greater than God, the church reaffirmed our humanity, restoring dignity to our lives. Such magnificence called for us to treat each other with a level of respect that was blatantly absent in our contact with Whites. Black men and women held leadership positions. They were given a chance not only to show off their skills and competence to do difficult jobs with expertise unrecognized in the other world, but they received the compliments and kudos for a job well done.

Similarly, church taught children how to behave and interact with adults. One such example I'll never forget occurred when my brother, sister and I, were walking to church from home, which was only a few blocks away. A woman said to my brother, "You're supposed to walk on the outside." She explained that all little boys were supposed to walk on the outside and let the girl walk on the inside. It never dawned on any of us to tell her to mind her own business, or say something sassy and ignore her. "Yes ma'am," my brother replied, and he immediately, did what she'd told him to. He didn't comply simply because he was a mannerable young man, but rather because this was a time when adults in the community could tell young people what to do. Even when a young person wished to rebel, she or he abided, indulging the adult's directive, as the completion of this communication protocol included an expectation of obedience. In this sense, all adults were your parents, and they took their pseudo-parental responsibility seriously, which was transmitted to the children who also took their roles as adults seriously.

In such aforementioned fashion, the church truly represented a place where socialization occurred. Which in hindsight was not surprising, given the historical nature of the roles the Black church served and consequently, the expectations the Black preacher was required to fill? Once viewed as a "nation in a nation" by E. Franklin Frazier (1969: 35), the church, in addition to acting as a social agency, an economic cooperation, and proponent for our educational development, also served as an arena of political involvement. There was no contradiction between our struggles for freedom and God's word delivered by the preacher who had been "called." In Black worship, they were one and the same. We always felt safe at church.

While I was too young to remember the NAACP-sponsored legal suits that dated back to the early 50s or of Rosa Parks' historic bus incident in Montgomery, Birmingham's twin, I was old enough to comprehend the discourse driving the Civil Rights Movement by 1960. (I had participated in enough fire drills generated by bomb threats in elementary school to know it wasn't empty rhetoric.) The Reverend Dr. Martin Luther King, Jr. was a household name. As the famed leader of the Civil Rights Movement, we put a lot of hope and trust in his non-violent strategy to achieve civil rights. Additionally, a lot of that same faith and optimism had been placed in then-president John Fitzgerald Kennedy to ensure the success of the Civil Rights Movement.

There was a widely held presumption that if you participated in the Civil Rights Movement then you possessed the character to represent Black interests and act as an advocate for Black people. Then as now, however, there were some individuals who were simply advocates for their own self-interests. This individualism had been one of the reasons that churches have lost the political punch they once held. Additionally, the Black church's popularity waned as other professions opened up to African Americans. They became doctors, lawyers, accountants, et cetera, and the new Black politicians and leaders emerged from these occupations and associations. "Many of these new and powerful representatives of the Black elite were not ministers, and owed no allegiance to the Black Church" (Marable, 2000: 198). The same can be said for Black civil rights organizations, such as the National Association for the Advancement of Colored People (NAACP). These organizations didn't move past the desegregation era to full economic and political equality.

Sixteenth Street Baptist Church was the hub of activity during this period of unrest and struggle. We would meet there for workshops designed to ensure that students and other people involved in the movement understood what they were marching for and why. On the morning of Sunday, September 15, 1963, the sanctity of the church was violated. Just before the 11:00 service at the 16th Street Baptist Church, a bomb exploded in the basement, killing Denise McNair, 11, and 14 year olds, Addie Mae Collins, Carole Robertson, and Cynthia Wesley.

James Taylor invited me to 16th Street Baptist Church that morning. He and I were good friends, so I would have gone, and no doubt, we would have been in that basement, too. I can't help but feel that but for the grace of God, I could have been one of those four girls murdered that morning. The only reason I didn't go was because my presence was required at my own church, Sardis Baptist where I was supposed to usher.

After the bombing, I understood even better how and why we resisted, demonstrated, marched and protested. My innards teemed with aspirations of freedom and all it entailed. While our hope didn't dissipate at this time, it cracked a little. Angry and outraged by the savage taking of young innocent lives, the people took to the streets in violent protests. Even though there were reports that the nation was in shock and enraged by the bombing, there was no understanding or empathy on the part of the city fathers. They met the protesters—with the blessing of then-Governor George Wallace and under the evil eyes of Sheriff Bull Connors—in a venomous show of force, with ferocious German Shepherds, blasting fire hoses that shot powerful streams of water, from those charged with upholding law and order, swinging billy clubs.

Watching the carnage on television, actually seeing the scope of the horrendous assault that was happening not far from your house, you realized a civil war that hadn't been declared was really going on. With bombs exploding all over the place and knowing that the chief of police was a member of the

Klan, made for a daunting feeling, especially as we had no protection from the outside world.

The police certainly couldn't be counted on. Even though they wore the "protect and serve" uniforms, they were more likely to serve us a protection reserved in death. The police who came into our neighborhood, as part of their regular patrol, never protected us. If the police came into the community someone might inevitably disappear. Someone might eventually be beaten up. Someone might ultimately be arrested for robbing a 7-11. Who knew what might have happened? But even not knowing with any degree of certainty, we didn't see their presence as a positive thing, never did and still don't.

We already knew that we were not safe in our homes, but now we had definitive proof that safety was no longer an assurance even in church. We were truly and wholly vulnerable to the devilish deeds of racism.

When the Sixteenth Street Baptist Church was bombed, it was as if the entire community was wounded. Even if you didn't know the families directly, it didn't matter because we were all family. I didn't know any of the four girls personally, but I knew the mother of one of them. Mrs. Robertson. She was my library teacher at Wilkerson. I can still recall her in class one day. She was just crying, and we were all sitting there in utter grief and despair, crying, too. How could any human, particularly a mother not feel the depth of anguish with another's loss of her child? There was no need to say anything. Besides, what could we have said that would have eased her agony? It was so painfully obvious that there was nothing we could do for her. We couldn't protect her. We couldn't help her. No one could bring back her child. No one could bring back our community. A group mourning took place.

The murders of those four young Sistahs weren't the only deaths that happened that day, and neither did the church bombing signify a new strategy in the warmongers plan for our complete elimination from society. Over 50 bombings occurred in Birmingham between 1947 and 1965, and two other Black youths were murdered that same day, September 15, 1963.

The ungodliness didn't stop with the church bombing. The nation's shock did little toward quelling our angst, or Birmingham's White power structure's persistence in maintaining the status quo of inequality. The seeds of hatred that had been planted in the sixteenth century grew like wildflowers across America.

I have almost reached the regrettable conclusion that the Negro's great stumbling block in our stride toward freedom was not due to the White Citizen's Council or the Ku Klux Klan. Instead, the finger of blame should have been pointed to the White moderate who was more devoted to "order" than to justice. For it was the White moderate who preferred a negative peace, the absence of tension, to a positive peace that signaled the presence of justice.

I understand Rebecca and Joan's shame and guilt, and my heart goes out to them. Even though their respective religious beliefs are a mystery to me, they had Christian hearts, a consciousness of fairplay, goodness, and justice. To realize as adults that they'd been raised racists, had it taught to them in their churches ... Well, I can but imagine the sense of betrayal they must feel, realizing that all they held dear, true and sacred was a lie.

When John F. Kennedy died, November 1963, I was going around the neighborhood selling, some kind of cleanser or detergent to raise money for band uniforms at Wilkerson Elementary. I went to one woman's house and caught her crying. She looked down at me and I told her what I was doing. She said, "Girl, I can't talk about it now, the President has been shot." I could tell she was sick with grief. She was crying, as were the other people in the house, watching the television.

At first, it struck me as unusual because people in the community always bought things from children. After realizing why people didn't want to talk to me about detergent, I went home too. My father and brothers and sister were at home glued to the TV. My mother was at work, but when she got home, she announced, "There's going to be a real mess now." It was quiet at our house. There were tears in my sister's eyes, astonishment on my older brother's face, while my father's expression was blank, as if he wasn't surprised and probably expected it.

People felt discouraged and were naturally worried and concerned about the future. We had taken a step forward, only to be snatched backwards with Kennedy's death. People were fearful again. Maybe things weren't going to get better. Maybe Malcolm X was right, and that thought truly frightened everyone.

When I look back on it, I don't remember a person talking in positive terms about Malcolm X. Everyone was afraid to follow his teachings, jolted by his hostile manner in demanding immediate freedom. More than that, he was a Muslim. The Black theology we heard every Sunday and during that moment of prayer as we planned marches didn't mix harmoniously with the rhetoric of the Nation of Islam, which we didn't understand or identify with. Consequently, people were not willing to embrace Malcolm X or his views. The familiar Christian way proposed by Dr. King was better.

When Dr. King died, I was at home watching television. I don't remember what we were watching because when they announced that he'd been shot, we started talking about it. I remember my mother's words: "Those low-down, dirty dogs killed him." We knew it had to be a White person because a Black person would never do something like that. Dr. King's death left a crater of anguish where high expectations resided. People dreaded the thought that past victories would be overturned without the vigilance of his presence.

Even in despair over his assassination, his death galvanized us, strengthened our resolve for freedom. It was as if everyone decided that we would not allow our progress to be impeded; that was not going to happen. We would no longer eat in the basement or drink from COLORED ONLY water fountains. Our minds were set: they killed him, but we weren't going back.

Amen!

Chapter Six

A World of Trouble

"A life lost: My brother and Vietnam"

There was about as much peace in Birmingham as there was in the world. Peace belonged where it was, in the dictionary, for it existed as an elusive concept, like a log drifting down the center of a wide, calm river, too far to capture from either side. **PROTEST** was the operative word of the day, for protests were visible, full of life and zeal, as one after another whipped across the country like a giant hurricane. At times, it seemed commonplace to me. In addition to those demonstrating for rights, there were those clamoring for peace as Vietnam had begun claiming lives faster than the country's mother could produce another child. And from Black families, she claimed a plenty.

But before Vietnam—never officially declared a war—a war of self-identity raged in the minds of young Black men. They couldn't take anymore of the emotional castration racism performed on their hearts. It was assumed, but never taken for granted that if they were American born, then inherently, they were Americans, backed and supported by a Bill of Rights. The damage done by 16th century claims of our inferiority, little better than superior monkeys, could not be undone. Even though some anthropologists warned those in the profession to act responsibly, by first weighing the effects of their scholarly discourse on the general populace, the admonition went unheeded.

The die cast, America refused to claim Black males as men. Ostracized, scorned, and rejected in their homeland, the only acceptance (for lack of a better word) came from the military to fight in some swamp-infested, alien land. Many took it as an opportunity to prove their loyalty to the country; many took it because it was their only opportunity. My oldest brother, Edward was one of Vietnam's victims.

During that time I was in high school. It was not only the Civil rights period, but the hippie movement, as well. I dropped out. I didn't do drugs, but I was into being different. One day I walked to the store without shoes and my dad was real upset because he said he worked hard to put shoes on my feet. But I felt that it was my life and if I didn't want to wear shoes I shouldn't have to and I didn't.

Anyway, my brother Edward came to the Top of Twenty-One, a restaurant at the Sheraton Hotel where my mother was a cook, and I, a waitress. He came to inform us that he had just joined the army. I was shocked. Some guys from the community had already been killed in Vietnam! In hindsight, I shouldn't have been daunted by his announcement for it was painfully obvious that he didn't know what to do once he graduated from high school. In hindsight, I remembered him as being hopeless.

Edward never believed he would have much of a life because he was not athletic. He once made a C in a class where I knew he could do better. I asked him why, to which he replied, "That's all they expect from me." So college never loomed like an eventuality in his mind, and he was without any skills, like carpentry or plumbing. He was just an average Black man who, in wartime, viewed the army as the best place for him. He had several friends who'd come to the same conclusion.

Early in school, Black men were given a message of their worthless value, except as a slave. Even by some Black people who told them by words or deeds that they were not going to amount to a hill of beans! As one reacted to a self-fulfilling prophesy, Edward accepted this doomsday prediction and prepared himself for a boring life. I guess that's why he volunteered for the army, an option I wished he hadn't taken.

The day that daddy took Edward to the airport, I couldn't bring myself to go. It was too much. I didn't want to say goodbye to him in the airport. He had on his uniform. He looked sharp. I said goodbye at home and he understood. I kept the image of him the week before he went to boot camp for safekeeping in my mind. He sold popcorn at Legion Field, and I helped him throw newspapers in the neighborhood.

His life changed significantly in boot camp at Fort Hood. Before long, they were sending him to Vietnam, and I fretted over whether I would ever see him again. We'd heard enough bad things about this place from the incendiary protests that divided the country to know he stood a good chance of not returning whole, if he returned at all. My daddy and brother went to see him off. My mother had to go to work. My sister was gone (she was a heroin addict). So he left and I didn't see him for over a year, but he wrote me from Vietnam.

I looked forward to the letters because I missed him. But most importantly if he wrote me I knew he was alive. I never shared the letters with my family. It was between my big brother and me. We could always depend upon one another: we had a special bond. In kinship structures discussed in anthropology, there has always been special mention of the relationship between brother-sister siblings. For me, my brother was the second male who contributed to my formation as a woman.

Edward gave me a look at how men viewed women because he talked about his girlfriends. He always had more than one (until Pam whom he married right after Nam). During the Christmas holidays we would ride on his motorcycle to deliver gifts to his girlfriends. Before we stopped at each house he would tell me what he liked about her. For instance, Linda made him laugh. She was funny and was always cracking jokes. I could see why he liked her. She was fun. Cynthia was a "hoochie mama." I think they had wild sex.

Before he went to Vietnam he married Pam in the gardens in Birmingham. Pam was sensible, fun loving and as he said, "wife material." He loved Pam. But then he had to leave for Nam.

Whenever he wrote me I would imagine him in the jungle. He wasn't the type to kill people. He was a paperboy and suddenly he was installed in the jungle with a rifle and told to kill children.

I received this letter from him while he was in Vietnam.

> Dear Janis,
> We landed at Cam Ram Bay where we went through orientation for a week. Charlie (nickname given the enemy) came in three days later. It lasted only a half-hour, but the damage was like a bomber had flown past. One whole side of the bay area was gone. I saw them die left and right. The saying that my drill sergeant told me that the survival of the fittest would come home. Time was on my side though. I had my youth to win my war within a war.
>
> After my stay there I went to the Land of the Eagle, Camp Eagle that is, home of the 101st Airborne Division. During that time I learned what survival was, with living in the boogie (jungle) for most of my eleven months. I became a boogie rat after that first firefight, and since that time, no cherry [new recruit] officer or enlisted man could tell me anything.
>
> We worked the highland mostly, which was all old A.O. (Area of Operation) until we came down the hill into the Ho Chi Min trail. We had to take two hills (301 and 310) on the map. It took four days to take those hills, and in that time we lost almost three companies of men, either wounded or killed in action. After the hill was taken, we were ordered to go back to Camp Eagle to get the Division back together with fresh cherries. I looked out at the bird and asked why, why did we go through all that fighting to take the objective just to leave and have it reclaimed again? No one answered then and no one will ever answer the main question of the year—why?
>
> Three months in the hole and there is no action, yet just moving from one A.O. to another. We are going up another of those small mountains when all at once we hear AK fire. We take cover, but then it stops just as quickly as it starts. We

move up until we come to the clearing. There on the ground is
the point man. His slack and the Platoon Leader are all dead. I
looked for what seemed like hours at those bodies until they
were loaded onto the bird. I know now what they meant when
they said live fast in Nam cause your days are short. We made
our home on top of that mountain that night knowing that all
hell would break lose before the next day begins.

It was three companies in the area that night, but if it were a
hundred I don't think anyone would have slept anyway. They
came at midnight with every kind of small arms that they had.
We were on the south end of the mountain which was the steep
side, but that didn't stop those gooks. They came in the hundreds. At this time our 8 in., 175, and mortar started a ring
around us. It looked like hell with nothing but shells bursting
all around us, but they came to die on and on for almost four
hours. We were fighting everywhere you look, there was either
gook or boogie rats dying. Death, that's what the night had---a
death wish for most because there was no help coming until the
fighting was over one way or the other. A little after four, it
stopped, just stopped. We didn't see them come, and we didn't
see them when they left.

We took a head count and there were 15 left out of 108 in
my company. We sent the wounded out first, then the dead. I
looked back down the side of the hill at the bodies stripped
down to nothing just like they would have done us if they had
won. Most were children, the average age around sixteen and I
thought about my brother.

Ninety days left, 90 more days and I will be going back to
the states. The day started with Gadikans bragging and I was
just too tired to hear any more. I told him to close his goddamn
mouth up or I'd close it for him. The fool got up and came at
me with nothing in his hands. All I did was wait until he was
five feet away and drew down on him with my M16 and aimed
at his head. He stopped dead in his tracks, not a word came out
of his mouth. There was sweat coming from his forehead like a
river in that short time. We looked each other down for that
sign of weakness that comes with fear. I finally asked do you
want to die or live, doing which time I flicked my 16 from
semi-automatic to automatic fire. He moved back one-step and
started to say something when the Platoon Leader stepped in
and gave me a direct order to put my rifle down. I told him he
could go down with Gadikans or get the fuck out of the way.
He slowly dropped his hand to the handle of his buck knife and
I slowly moved my rifle from one head to the other. I already
saw him throw that knife and kill a gook, but I'm not about to
let the same thing happen to me. We looked each other straight
in the eye waiting for that sign that will tell who will live and

who will die. He moved his hand away from the buck knife and went back to where he was sitting not saying a word. I said to Gadikans it's just me and you now so what will it be boy. He now moved forward a step, but stopped, he knew if he came any closer I would kill him. He slowly stepped back and said maybe next time.

Sleep comes quick to me with midnight being my time to take over on watch. I'm almost at home doing nothing but hanging on the corner trying to make ends meet when the first shell comes in. It hit about 25 feet from my hole. There is a cry then nothing. The radioman called in to the company to say we are under attack. Two more shells came in now but there is no small arms fire that usually comes with the rocket attack. After five minutes on the radio the platoon leader found out that the company forward operator had called in the mortar rolls for our night defense since we were in a hot area of operation. We had a head count and there was only one person hurt and one killed. That was Gadikans with a hole in his head the size of softball. There was a heavy fog that had come in early so we had to wait until the next day before we could airlift him out. This was a time when I felt nothing, no emotion; no feeling was coming out of my mind. I knew I had joined the ranks of the few then. To see a man lose his life and not have any kind of lost mixture of feeling was the end of the line for me. I would turn to drugs in the future. Hard core all the way, no more grass, just anything else to put in my arms ...

I got more letters from him that I cherished, even though they brought despair. I grew immensely tired and frustrated of him being there and those letters reminding me of where he was. He liked to write and I sent him pictures.

My brother came home a decorated hero, having earned the National Defense Service Medal, Air Medal, Army Commendation Medal, and the Vietnam Service Medal with two Bronze stars and a Vietnam Campaign Medal. Yet and still, Edward was never the same after Vietnam. The medals seemed meaningless. They certainly didn't provide the impetus of an attempt at mainstream life. He returned more withdrawn and somber, in silent conflict. He painted his room Black and played a lot of music that I wasn't familiar with, like Chicago and Santana. I loved the music. As a matter of fact Santana's Abraxas (remastered in 1999) was the first album I ever bought. My brother smoked a lot of pot in his room. We could smell the incense throughout the house, but no one bothered him. He got jobs as a waiter, but you could tell he wasn't happy. Eventually he and his wife got an apartment together, but happiness remained elusive.

If there had ever been hope secretly harbored in his soul, it had gone up in the flames of the wars he fought.

Chapter Seven

Feminism in Absentia

"Too Many Enemies to Fight"

The marches and demonstrations and protests against Viet Nam were all aggressive struggles fought to achieve goals that every participant believed would make America a better country, one that truly and wholly lived up to its promise as the "home of the free and land of the brave." However, there also existed a silent courage that no man, black or white, heard. A harmful, yet subtle phenomenon, it appeared in every black segment of every black community in America; however, it went largely ignored, as all energies and emphasis were invested in one goal, and that was achieving racial equality.

Because black people equated racism with loss of manhood, it was reasoned that if we got rid of racism, then black men would take their rightful position. This reasoning gave rise to a hypothesis of gender hierarchy whereby it would resemble a parallel that placed black men on the same plane as white men, with the contention that in such an equation the black man would then be dominate like the white man.

The failure of this logic went ignored, for even if you worked on one hierarchy, another hierarchy remained to be addressed. It appeared that women were seen as inconsequential. This hypothetical paradigm featuring black men juxtaposed to white men never took the woman's, black or white, place into consideration. As if the women were non-existent in the higher cause of equality for which both fought and died to achieve?

This schism between genders was visible in my community. For instance, there was men's work, like the milkman or postman, and then there was women's work. During this time, and even before, never in our wildest dreams did we think there could be milk-*women* or post-*women*. It was taken for granted by both black women and men that these were men's jobs.

Most of the men were blue-collar laborers who worked in the steel mills in Sippecoe. A few were doctors, dentists and other types of professionals and naturally, there were a lot of ministers. A black policeman was a rarity, if one existed in Birmingham at all. There were quite a few black businessmen who owned stores in the community or in the black downtown. Some were teachers, but often women held these positions: it was seen as a more appropriate occupation for a wife.

Largely, women were cooks, domestics, nurses, teachers, clerks, et cetera. In a sense, women did work considered 'typical' of women today. Some women worked at home. For instance, Mrs. Stokes, who lived across the street from us, was a seamstress. She made most of the dresses my sister and I wore. Mrs. Stokes was really busy before the beginning of the school year because she sewed for a lot of people.

However, women seemed to like the setup, for it meant that their men were working, which allowed them to continue doing women's work. No one advocated equality between black women and men. It was unequal, and everyone seemed to view it as the natural order. Simply, women were not considered leaders; even though, they were always organizing for one thing or another.

Nearing the end of Civil Rights and at the crest of the Black Power movements, a new struggle emerged in this country. Another group felt denied opportunities and choices. It was created and largely composed of white women who took their swing at the piñata of America's sweets. Called the feminist movement, it addressed the need for freedom and equality of a different kind from the hierarchy white men who held dominion over all. There seemed to be an attempt to create a new hierarchy with white women at the top with white men. Women of color were still relegated to the bottom. These women weren't a part of the feminist movement. It was considered a White Women's Movement.

Black women didn't buy into the White Women's Movement. These already active women denounced feminism, believing that race consciousness was significantly more important than gender issues. After all, they had been aware of race and racism since infancy, and shared the same daily doses of degradation as their men. Many died knowing nothing else.

Neither could they get a white job, regardless if a white man or white woman held the position. Neither could they earn the salary paid a white man or a white woman. Neither were water fountains, restrooms, nor restaurants labeled by gender: race determined admittance or acceptance. Consequently, neither black woman nor man could drink, pee, or eat from places deemed for WHITES ONLY.

Living lives of constant vigilance to matters pertaining to race and racism, Black women were imbued with a race consciousness. This painful awareness demanded that they operate from a position of "we", meaning Black Women and Black Men. From enslavement and beyond emancipation, Black women knew that they, as well as their men were oppressed. Be it on the Underground

Railroad or a bus ride, facing capture and brutality alike, they shared in every mien of human and social injustice.

Besides, the proverbial Miss Anne didn't mind black women working for them as cooks, maids, seamstresses, caretakers and raisers of their children. Why, she might even have loaned her car to ensure that her black worker could make it to work on time when other modes of transportation were for whatever reason not possible. But she never before broached the task of dismantling segregation and its harsh and unfair treatment of black women.

What was the point in black women fighting for the rights of women when they lacked the primary qualifications obvious in the color of their skin? The doors of opportunities were slammed shut in their collective black faces and the walls of equality collapsed around their black bodies.

"No" to NOW. If liberation were to be won, it would be as a union, Black Women and Black Men struggling together. Hence, sexism, an inhuman act as heinous as racism, hardly registered on the scale of concern. "We" didn't have time to deal with sexism while racism still existed. And naturally there existed within this rationale the thought that if a black woman wanted to deal with issues of gender bondage, she must be a lesbian. Consequently, NOW which didn't nor does now deal with racism or black women, never developed a toehold in the black community.

Finding the door wide open on the opportunity to struggle for equality as participants in both the Civil Rights and Black Power movements, black women walked through that door blindly, without a second-thought. Unfortunately, once the perception of that path had been crossed, with the firm belief that equality had been achieved, black women walked into another closed door, one closer to home.

It offered a lesson in the value of feminism that Black women had heretofore ignored. That a feminist consciousness was absent, or rather subjugated to a bigger cause, made it easy for a story, such as mother's to occur. The following is a transcription of what I just recently learned about my family for the first time.

. . . My name is Alice Hutchinson. I'm married now. It's all about my family life when I was a little girl. First, I want to tell you my daddy's name was John B. Williams. My momma was Annie Williams, and she had four brothers, Harry, one called John D., Steven, and the one I loved, called Big Bubba. His name was Brad, but we never did call him by his name. Two sisters, Ann and my baby sister, Ossie. We were a very happy family when we were little. It don't seem like what I'm fixin to tell you is true. It's hard to believe, but believe me it's for real.

It started when we were little kids. I don't know why my daddy did my momma like that. I guess just low down, and havin all these children by my momma wasn't enough. He had to mess around with another woman and that didn't matter. All he had to do was leave momma, not try to kill her. This was what he did to my momma.

We were little kids, in the sixth grade. I will remember that always. It was in the 1930s. One day, I will always remember this day, we were sitting down in the kitchen listening at the radio because that's all we had to do. We heard our momma scream. Just scream. You know little kids they hear their momma scream and they go and running.

We got up, me and Ann (her sister who was only 9 months older than her). We went running in the house. Momma was just about dying. She just grabbed us and was groaning. All we could hear momma say was "*doctor*." We knowed where to go.

We left out that house, Ann and myself, running like the wind. We run all the way to the doctor's office, off a field of cuccabugs. We was bloody when we got there. We were so out of breath we could barely speak. He grabbed us and knew who children we was. He said, "*These Ann's children.*"

He said, "*What's the matter with Ann?*" We told him that she was slobbering and gagging and eating lard. When we said eating lard. He knowd it had to be some kind of poison. So he throwd a lot of stuff into the bag and threw us in the car.

He got us back to the house and the first thing he did was gave her some kind of solution that made her vomit. You see. What happened was my daddy had put cyanide in my momma's medicine.

This was the first time that he tried to kill her. Momma didn't know her medicine was poisoned. Like she always do, daddy always knew how momma takes her medicine. Wine and cocrin. It was like that 3S tonic. You got women having children to take it to build their body. Momma always did keep wine and cocrin. He put this poison in my momma medicine. She used to shake it up; she never did use a spoon, she would shake this bottle every morning and take her three swallows. And we knowed this by watching her every day. So that morning she took that medicine it was poisoned some how or another. "Momma must have knowed that medicine was poisoned cause the minute that she drank that medicine she grabbed that lard. She grabbed a hand of lard and just ate it, just pushed it down in her mouth in her stomach. Then she started vomiting.

He didn't even have to ask her what happened. He got her medicine and smelled it to his nose. He shook his head. He said, "*Lord have mercy. Red Jim did this.*" That's what everybody called my daddy cause he was whiter than he was black. He told momma do not to take any more medicine at the house. Say if she got anymore medicine to hide it.

. . .

Another time he tried to kill momma with voodoo. Janis I know it's hard for you to believe but that stuff works. He killed another man with it but I'll tell you about that later. Well momma started getting real weak. She was a hard workingwoman and suddenly she started sitting a lot. She never said that anything was wrong. One day she just passed out on the front porch. We called my brothers Bubba, Harry, John, and Steven to help us put her in bed. She woke up and said no need to call the doctor. I'm probably just tired. She just stayed in bed all day. The next day we got the doctor to look at her but he couldn't find anything wrong. They didn't do a whole lot of blood work and test back then you know. We told one of momma's friends Ms. Cherry about it and she said she saw our daddy at Jessie Mae's house, a hoodoo woman. That's when we knew he had done something to momma. We went to another hoodoo woman; I forget her name, because the one who put it on her won't take it off. This woman said we had to find what he used to put the hex on her. He had to use something that belongs to her like hair or nails. We searched the house but couldn't find anything that looked like it had been gathered. You knowd like a ball of hair wrapped in cloth. Momma was weak but she would still go outside to check on the animals. You know we had chickens and ducks and make sure we were feeding them. Then we all realized that every time she walked off the porch she would get weak and sometimes fall. We looked under the steps and there was a ball of her hair wrapped in cloth that had blood on it. He used her menstrual blood and hair and got the woman to put some kind of hex on it. We took it to the other hoodoo woman and she burned it. After that momma got better.

The last time he tried to kill her, he was bold. He took a shotgun and shot her in the hip on the front porch in front of us. Blood was all over everybody. We dragged her in the house while my brothers protected her from him and we ran to get the doctor. When we told him what happened, he came back to the house and got the bullet out right there. He said Red Jim's gonna kill your momma, and left. Back then the police wouldn't get involved in anything like that. It was all right for a man to kill a woman and we knew it because it happened to other women. Papa Jim wanted to be with another woman so he just decided to get rid of momma. He knew the police weren't going to arrest him because he was in with them. Papa sold moonshine besides having the lumber mill so no one bothered him. Besides his mother was a white woman, Anne Robertson, and their family would help him although they never visited us and we didn't visit them. Even today none of the older people like to talk about that side of the family. My sister and my brothers decided we were tired of this and we were going to stop it. One day when he came home my brothers grabbed him and took him into the barn. We had some burlap bags. We were going to chop him up and throw him in the lake. My brothers had his head on the chopping block and were about to chop his head off with an axe when momma came in and said, "Don't do it. I don't want my children going to jail."

We let him up, but my brothers told him he better get and he did. He took his money and moved to Buffalo, New York where he had friends but no family. His family didn't like him.

When I was young, I knew that my grandfather lived in Buffalo, but I never knew why until my mother told me this story. He lived there for over twenty years. He moved to Birmingham when I was around nine years old because he had diabetes and both of his legs had been amputated. But before coming to Birmingham, he went to live in Tuskegee with momma's youngest brother, Steven. Again, he was forced to leave because people claimed he killed a man with voodoo.

I used to believe there was something to voodoo when I was little. My grandfather had the power to turn on the lights by clapping his hands. This was before *Clap-On*. My aunt said that he probably crawled out of the bed in the middle of the night and rewired the house.

My mother hated her father. When I asked her what he did for a living, she replied, "Every damn thing." One day he got angry with my mother and put a hex on her. When she walked out of the house, she fell down the stairs. Of course, everyone thought it was due to the hex.

My grandfather was a mean man. His hatefulness clearly explained why my mother married my father. The compote opposite of her father, her husband was the most gentle, mild-mannered person you could ever want to meet. He never spoke a harsh word, didn't possess a violent bone in his body, and lived the stereotype of a hard-working, family man. He was a great father and I miss him dearly.

I recorded the story because my mother wanted us to know, but it was too painful for her to tell again and again. After she told the story the first time to me, she looked at me with tears in her eyes and said she had never thought about it as abuse or domestic violence until now.

During that time, all married women expected to be abused: it was part of being married. It would be a mistake to assume that only black women of my mother's generation held this view. Young black women in a study I conducted on condom use between 1995 and 1997 bore witness to this long lasting perception. The results showed more conclusively than rhetoric how racism and sexism have devalued black women, the carriers of our culture.

The aim of the study was to understand the social meaning of condom use so that appropriate HIV/AIDS intervention and education could be developed for young adult African-American women. African-American women were solicited at a local gangsta rap nightclub, which I fictitiously named, Club X. With a clientele composed mainly of young, under-30 crowd, it was a sport's bar with a lot of TVs including a big screen and pool tables. A wide variety of people, ranging from students, engineers, postal workers and those looking for work went to the club.

It was not unique among black nightclubs in Houston, but rather similar to others in terms of age and sex composition, and percentage of nonwhites (small numbers of whites and Hispanics). What was different, however, was the great volume of gangsta rap - - a degrading metamorphosis of "signifying" and "playing the Dozens" where the aim was to verbally destroy your opponent or a woman - - music played (Geneva Smitherman, 1977, *Talkin and Testifyin: The Language of Black America*). Today, gangsta rap is described as the controversial type of music, whereby the rappers espouse themes of killing, use of guns, extremely derogatory statements about women, and explicit sexual statements. In addition, the music has portrayed realistic views of life in the African-American community, providing a representation of what it is like to be black in a white dominated American society. I was introduced to the club by one of my students who became HIV infected while attending the club. She dated a guy named Blue, a drug dealer who coaxed her into having sex with his friends.

I went to the club around midnight on the weekends at around ten on Mondays, popularly known as ladies' night. It was hard going there at midnight. That was past my bedtime. All of my friends thought it was great that I was doing research in a club. I had to try to fit in and not look too conspicuous, for in addition to being older than the typical crowd; my dreadlocks were out of place and style with a female clientele most of whom which had processed hair. Another source of discomfort came from the drug dealers who had their own areas in the club: everyone knew who they were, where they were, and how to spot them. Blue, for instance, had a corner of the room that belonged to him. One night while I was in the club a drug dealer pointed at me and asked, "Who is that?" My student went over to explain that I was doing research and was not an undercover narcotics cop. Cleared from suspicion; the dealer bought me a drink.

Women danced with men in the club as if they were engaged in sex. I called it sexual dancing. Sometimes they danced on the floor as they grinded each other. Women drank large jugs of beer like the guys. One woman explained the reason, stating that it was "to let the men know that we're just as strong as them." Sometimes I saw pregnant girls drinking these jugs.

The music was definitely demeaning to women. I talked to the DJ about it and he said the women usually requested it. One night he played a song with the lyrics "women ain't nothing but bitches and hoes", and it was as if everybody in the club knew the words (but me, of course) and sung along with the record. I wanted to run out, but then I wouldn't have been able to recruit women to inter-

view. There was a raid one night, and everyone had to get on the floor. The police were looking for contraband and took some people to jail. Did I forget to
mention that people sometimes smoked marijuana in the club while on the
dance floor?

The women for my study were often recruited in the restroom. As many were
talking about men anyway, it seemed a good time to talk about condoms (not
HIV). I signed them up and later called to set up the interview.

It was disheartening to realize the low self-esteem that many young women
have. For them, the relationship was more important than the risk of HIV. Using
condoms meant that you were not in a monogamous relationship. Women didn't
want to admit it, however, even if they knew it was true—a macho-female kind
of thing. 'Men have the power' was a theme echoed among them. This was
shown when I went to the house of a woman where I had already setup an interview. Her boyfriend called and told her to stop the interview until he found out
what it was about. I had to get on the phone and explain it to him in a way that
he wouldn't think that I was trying to take away his power. She had to get permission from him, which she did, before the interview could continue.

Concerning infidelity and condom use, one woman stated, "I'm concerned.
I'm very concerned. We don't use condoms. But you know he carries them,
which is fine. You know the thought that he carries them is good but then it's not
good because you know. But we don't. The reason why? I just feel like because
we go together although I know we should. But I know it's really not like that. I
feel that I trust him even though in the back of my mind I know I shouldn't, but I
do. I trust him. I feel old fashion. I feel that if you're in a relationship that's it,
and we've been together off and on for four or five years. So I just feel that I
trust him and when we do date we are together. It's important but I just don't
worry about it, you know."

At the beginning of a relationship people would use condoms and get tested,
but after they considered themselves in a relationships, they stopped using condoms.

"When we first met, it didn't come up. After it seemed like we were going to
be together it came up. I said no; I don't think it's necessary because we're supposed to be so serious and if it's going to be just you and I, I felt like we should-
n't have to."

The aforementioned scenarios were played out in a context of gender imbal-
ance and racism within a low-income environment. Each of the women's stories
sadly revealed that she had more important issues than sexually transmitted diseases to consider: economic survival and holding on to the one they loved took
precedent over their own personal health and welfare. Women's perception of a
potential sexual partner and husband have been based on economics and perceived faithfulness. However, boyfriends and husbands were not expected to be

faithful. Nevertheless, they made a trade off, risking their health for love and the enhanced social status of having a man.

The existence of this tragedy did not magically appear like a unique phenomenon or a fad of the 90s that shows promise of disappearing in the new millennium. A history of long standing abuse, damaging to both black women and men has seemingly been cemented in place. Black people invested in the sexist way of thinking when they bought into making black men equal to white men in terms of domination, failing to see that it was just another form of power relationships. It was as if we'd forgotten the impact of power and history to play havoc with our lives.

The history of domestic violence in black homes began long before the Civil Rights Movement. In fact, it was can be traced back to slavery. Black men, frustrated when 'Massa' raped black woman, (from whence the term 'motherfucker' originated) forcing him to stand idly by and watch with acceptance, he then took his feelings of utter powerlessness out on her, compounding the brutality black women suffered. After Civil Rights, which resulted in a rise of laws that seemed to open doors for black participation, the perception of equality enlarged the heads of black men.

When the reality of every Supreme Court decision that had favored fair and equal treatment but not separate decisions fell through, dreams exploded in our heads, but black men took it more personally. (It should be noted that the word equality has not been mentioned in a one of those legal documents.) Their dreams literally went up in smoke as the truths revealed that the laws of equality were for the books, dead documents, no more valuable than fodder for the fireplace. And black men followed the noxious cloud by either abandoning their families, or if they stayed, taking their disappointments out on the very women who marched and protested right alongside them.

It spelled out in plain English, as never before, that equality was not meant for black women. Equality was taken to mean the liberation or freedom of *black manhood*, and black women need not apply. Exploited as workers, as blacks, and as women, this triple oppression black women faced, escaped black males entirely (Marable, 2000). In essence, Black men failed to tend to the carriers of black culture (black women) after Emancipation as carefully as the white man tended the black woman's ability to produce more property for work on his plantation.

We acted as if we faced a problem of algebraic equality in search of 'n', the unknown. But 'n' was there all the time: the same ideology, created in the sixteenth century that oppressed black men and women collectively was the same system of patriarchy, racism and heterosexism—white privilege that picked us apart. As Barbara Jordan once said, "I was not included in the "We the people." This same exclusion existed for black women who experienced this blow from three bullets. With few exceptions, Black men didn't see our pain or notice the destructive residual outcomes trickling down to threaten the Black Family.

And it has left an unfortunate legacy, especially to our young generation of black women, and not just those from a low-income environment where one may think that a more enlightened environment would wash away the ills. As there has been no concerted form of resistance since the Black Power Movement, many of us have misinterpreted the career gains and personal economic growth as progress, viewing them as new opportunities, a road traveled before.

We can no longer afford to be fooled by the notion of 'politically correct' behavior, which has become the *modus operandi* of this new and subtle form of racism plaguing our world. This made it easy to believe that assimilation was a college degree away. The propaganda of achievement have seemed complete and victorious to those in denial of the countermovement successfully launched by conservatives who have instituted subtraction equations. Affirmative Action has almost become an archaic concept, barely able to climb from the one-dimensional pages of Webster's Dictionary while the Glass Ceiling, albeit recent terminology has persisted in practice.

Aware that race remained an issue, many women haven't understood how nor developed strategies to cope with it beyond clumsy, passive responses that left them feeling frustrated and angry, and even paranoid about those feelings. Such reactions have resulted in ignoring or turning a blind eye to the racism targeted to them specifically. Instead, many have simply preferred to view it as an extension of the slight against black men. These young Sistahs have gone to the extreme, defending black men, again ignoring or failing to realize the peculiar intrapersonal game of self- victimization.

Recently, I heard the following in a focus group with black female students on campus when we discussed their views about domestic violence. They seemed to justify it by talking about how black men have been beaten down and that women should be understanding and not leave the black man because black women should hold up the black man.

"I think that society today has put black men at the bottom of the totem pole," said one young woman. "Society has just fundamentally stripped them . . . We just live in basically a white man's world, we live in a white man's society, and we live in a world that is afraid of black men. And because of that, they have systematically tried to destroy the momentum of black men. It has happened since we have been in America as black people. And I think black women have to be more sensitive to that because even as black women, we have not experienced, you know, the level of just being demeaned the way they have."

Another contended, "I think it would be important for us in a relationship to try to stand up and try to pull them up and build them up and be more sensitive to what's going on in their day-to-day lives. I can't think of any other color or any other race in America that has to deal with what black men have to deal with."

On the subject of relationships between black women and men, one of the women declared, "I'm gonna support him, you know, of course. But he's not going to run over me, and boss me around, if he's not being what a man is, you know? A man is not going to misuse his woman's trust and his woman's love, just for his own advantage, you know? He's gonna try to lead her in the right direction, and if she submits to him, she's gonna be submitting to him for the good of herself, as well as the good of him. Not just to make him you know, feel that, you know, he's a man. It's gonna have to be some incentives behind that submission. I mean, I'm gonna tell him what he needs to do, but not actually, what I'm saying, being bossy, or you know, I'm not gonna beat him or nothing like that. (laughs) But I think, I think the woman is there to give him ideas, to stand behind him, and when he's going wrong, be there to be like say, That's not right. You need to think that out"...

That Black women need to be more aware of the role sexism, both exploitive and victimizing, played in their lives (myself included) was evident in a story told me by my Mother. Both my aunts and grandmother, nor my mother mentioned it during my childhood: it was a family secret. Now told, it provided some insight about how black women thought about their place in a world dominated by men. In *How Capitalism Underdeveloped Black America* (2000), Manning Marable wrote, "Capitalist patriarchy, combined with racism, shackles the majority of Black women more firmly to the process of exploitation than any group of black men."

Black women are underpaid, do not get the promotions, reach glass ceilings faster than men and are more likely to live in poverty than men. Domination of the economic system by white males has resulted in not only oppression, but poverty for minorities, especially women because the capitalist patriarchy is coupled with sexism. One consequence of male domination of the money industries and businesses is relegation of minority women to low paying jobs as shown by my mother's experiences in hotels where she had to train white men, who were the head chefs, to do her job (and make more money than her). Because women are devalued in capitalist patriarchy they must resort to other means of subsistence for themselves and their children. The result is that women need males not only for companionship but, for economic survival. Women believe, then, that they must be attached to a man in order to have money to live. They cannot make it on their own. They earn less and have children, so they need this attachment in order to survive. As a result, they are vulnerable to exploitation. They put up with objectionable behavior in men because they need their economic support and men know that they need this support.

It would be deceitful of me not to mention the black feminist efforts of the likes of bell hooks, Barbara Smith, Paula Sue Giddings, Angela Davis, and

Deborah King, prominent in the struggle to conceptualize *Revolutionary Black Feminism*, in both theory and practice. Partly in response to the white feminist movements' omission of racial and gender issues of concern to black women, this Black Feminism has emerged to foster a concrete liberation of working class and poor women.

However, I find shortcomings in the concept; it doesn't go far enough to embrace our entire community. Although there is a simultaneous struggle for equality between the genders as well as between black communities and the larger society, Black women cannot be feminist because feminism works to our collective disadvantage. If equality is truly sought, it promises a battle that can only be won with our collective participation of men, women, and children. If a woman has to separate her interest to do one job successfully—freeing or finding equality for herself—then she hasn't the energy to fight the battles of those remaining. It is incumbent on us all to do what is necessary to liberate the Black community, women, children, and men.

Womanism, sometimes referred to as Black Feminism, has the power to accomplish that end, as it considers not just the rights and goals of black women, but the black community. Personally, the concept of Womanism has represented a similar intent of Black Feminism, without advocating patriarchy as paramount. Taking a holistic stand, in addition to responding to the advancement of women, it is inclusive of community, rights or equality, as well as recognizing and, for many, respecting patriarchy within the black community (if one feels the need to do that). Womanism does not position itself to mean that black women are equal to white men or white women in terms of domination and oppression. In other words, it has not realigned the gender hierarchy. It is not devoid of sexism but it does eliminate racial hierarchies and is not the traditional gender hierarchy. In other words, men and women have been positioned to enjoy equal and respected footing, while the black community benefits as a full-citizen in American life.

Chapter Eight

From Embryo to Neophyte

"If you're black, America is like an uncle who
paid your way through college but molested you."
Chris Rock, 2004

Going to college was the only viable option in the diagnosis for success that most Black parents prescribed for their children. At my house, the adage," Don't do as I do, but do as I say" reigned supreme. It was juxtaposed to "don't get in trouble" and "don't get pregnant." What we were supposed to do was "go to college and get a degree."

Since the days of Booker T. Washington (founder of Tuskegee Institute in 1881, from where my father earned his degree) Black people believed that if we lifted ourselves up through hard work and education, then acceptance as first class citizens would be ours. We have held on to this philosophy despite the numerous contradictions that prove it to be a fallacy. W.E.B. DuBois realized early on that education would not solve the race issue in this country, which in part explained why he thought that we should go back to Africa.

Nevertheless, Black mothers wanted it for their daughters in particular because they were thoroughly familiar with the options of employment deemed suitable for females. I had the blessing of having seen it for myself when I worked in hotels and restaurants. While a Black woman with a degree served as a twofer on the scrolls of affirmative action, an uneducated Black woman could count on the likelihood of double mistreatment.

George Wallace once stood in the door and declared that "Negroes" would never attend the University of Alabama. Well, here we were, maybe about a hundred or so, but you only ever saw about 40 or 50 of us, and me, too. We were like an island in the middle of the ocean. Only, the water surrounding us was White, instead of blue. We were separate from them. In order to survive emotionally and psychological, we supported one another, forming an extended family.

It was my first experience from home. I lived in Martha Parham Dormitory and experienced all the pressures, pleasures, and nuisances of a freshman. There was nothing unusual about being the only Black person in the class. We didn't think anything of it because that was simply the way it was. Initially, I was reticent to ask questions in class. It occurred to me later that if I needed to know something, I had damn well better ask. My questions were answered like anyone else's.

I took fifteen hours my first semester. Even though I had always been an A and B student, I was nervous about college. I didn't want to flunk out and have to go home. I made an 'F' on the first exam for every test that I took. I was devastated. I went home on the weekend and told my mother and she told me to go back and just do my best. I talked to all of my professors to see what I was doing wrong. I had to learn to take better notes. Not to write down everything, but to figure out key points. I changed my study habits and studied more. By the end of the semester, I walked away with B's and C's. It was a relief. I just passed my first semester in college.

To tell you the truth, my fours years of undergrad at Alabama were full of partying. We had one everyday. We went to class and studied, for sure, but from around noon to three, we could be found playing bid whisk in the university center. And there were some great concerts for only $2. We went to see everybody who came: Jimmy Buffet, Santana, Ramsey Lewis, the Allman Brothers, the Rolling Stones with Stevie Wonder, Chicago, Stanley Turrentine. Before they became famous, we saw the Atlanta Rhythm Section and Nitty Gritty Dirt B for free. One time, to my knowledge, the police took pictures of everyone at the concert. They seemed to think that anyone attending those free concerts was some type of alien species or criminals. It was easy to be put on lists. I subscribed to the Socialists Newspaper. When I went to pick one up (everyone had to go to the mail room to pickup mail) the woman told me that "they" had put my name on a list because I subscribed to a communist newspaper. I was just a student trying to learn about things. As any typical collegian, I also tried different religions, from Bahai to Islam, and eventually, atheist, only to revert back to the faith I'd been born into, Christianity.

It was Bear Bryant country and it was not unusual to see Joe Namath riding down University Boulevard in his White convertible Bonneville. He also owned a restaurant in town. (I can't tell you how the food was because I never ate there, couldn't afford it anyway.)

As music saved my sanity in high school, I relied on it again, playing the clarinet in the Million Dollar Band. Band membership, among other things, offered the opportunity to travel to different cities. It was difficult practicing every evening, but the games provided inevitable good times. When we played in the Orange Bowl, a friend of mine and I arrived late at the airport and missed the plane. We had to arrange our own travel. It was a hassle, as was getting reimbursed, but it was worth it.

Under the watchful eyes of thousands of people brought about fantastic feelings. One of them was pride. It was a moment of freedom, for there was little time to think when you're on the field performing. You had to know your music and react automatically to keep up with the movement of the routine.

Sometimes, the crowd was as rough as the football players who played the game. In Tennessee, they threw oranges on the field at us. Some people were down right rude over a game. The worst defeat for us that I remember occurred when we played Nebraska and a Black player, Johnny Rogers, had a stellar day. He kept running down the field scoring touchdowns. I think they beat us by over 40 points. Like Steely Dan sang, "Alabama's a winner, but sometimes we lose."

While the band offered an enjoyable outlet, classroom learning was a different matter. Not that I didn't enjoy learning. It was what I had to learn that made my stomach turn. I was never more appreciative of Carter G. Woodson for writing *The MisEducation of the Negro*, than during my academic experience at Alabama. The prevailing discourse in my discipline, anthropology, represented a regurgitation of the racist dogma used to justify slavery in America and the colonialization of Africa dating back to the fifteen hundreds.

It has always been a given that if a student intended to pass the course, she had to learn the information on which she would be tested. The student assumed that the information given was correct or true. However, I had to learn some things I didn't believe. It became downright arduous having the so-called inferiority of my race thrown in my face in practically every anthropological construct I studied. I had come from Birmingham, where racism embodied a cultural way of life, and here, they were teaching it—lock, stock, and barrel. Teachers regurgitated its evolutionary path from origins to modern-day thinking, and I had to learn this prejudicial discourse. It was a hellavu trade off for a degree.

Imagine the others in my class who have gone on to disseminate such nonsense that Blacks never contributed to civilization. This idea has been examined extensively; however, the subject refused to disappear, from the 1600s into the 1800s. For example, in 1817 George Cuvier argued that Blacks did not create Egyptian civilization, but rather Europeans who had large brains created it (Stocking, 1982). In *Crania Aegyptica*, Samuel George Morton argued that only Caucasians developed a great civilization and that the social position of Blacks ... "in ancient times was the same that it now is, that of servants and slaves" (Morton, 1844:66). By showing that Blacks had been slaves since ancient times, Morton implied that their subjugation was inevitable and natural.

These studies indicated that Blacks were cursed and lacked civilization. It also gave a scientific explanation for their lack of culture, attributable to their stage of development (unilinear evolution) based on physical evidence in the bones examined by then Harvard University professor, Carlton Coon. The bones were ranked based upon what was considered superior (White features and culture) versus inferior, Black physical features and culture (physical anthropology). He believed that the different races evolved separately and that in this process some races, Whites, had evolved more than the other groups. To him, over two million years ago the races separated, with no gene flow between them. In a way, he considered the different races to be different species. His argument was that since Whites evolved the most, they were most intelligent and had the "highest" civilization.

It was setup to prove what they believed to be true: Whites were/are superior to Blacks. But in 1972, this racist ideology blazed the halls of academia across the country. I felt the bitterness born during my childhood in Birmingham slither like a poisonous snake through my veins. But I squashed it dead as I'd learned to do from my father. Besides, as an undergrad, I didn't think I could argue with people such as the eminent, prestigious Coon who espoused this garbage. When we discussed his theory in class, critique hardly ever entered into the discussion, as if it was an open and shut case of reality. I wanted to argue, but all I could say was that I didn't believe it, being feeble in knowledge to explain why. After all, they seemed to have the evidence to support it. I understood better than ever before the meaning of the old saying that "you have to learn to crawl before you could walk."

White superiority was a tired refrain, constantly repeated and reaffirmed as if they didn't want us to ever forget it. I kept silent with my gut feelings that countered White people's belief that their civilization was better than anyone else's, even when they were claiming that they were more intelligent than Blacks. It certainly wasn't obvious in class. There were some really dumb White students. Sometimes I wondered how they ever got into the university.

The second thing that I had to learn, and again did not believe was that behavioral and mental abilities were basically genetic in origin. This too seemed like a setup, but once again, I came up short. I simply had to hold fast to my belief against this ethnocentric perception that merely reaffirmed the history of racism in America.

Gene theories, allegedly irrefutable scientific studies, served the goals of racist ideologists although they were countered in the 1930s by Otto Klineberg who showed that northern Blacks were more intelligent or scored higher on IQ tests than southern Whites (Klineberg, 1935). Also, Blacks in the north scored higher than Blacks in the south. What this actually revealed was that social environment pertaining to access to a quality education appeared important. Furthermore, one needed to pose the question—what were they testing for?

Achieved learning was revealed through IQ tests while intelligence is the potential to solve novel situations (potential for learning). Pitting them together was like trying to determine which was better, apples and oranges, overlooking the meaning of IQ tests. We cannot measure intelligence, only achieved learning. Even in achieved learning though, Klineberg showed that Blacks were capable of learning just as much as Whites. It was a small blessing, most submerged by racist dogma failed to see that the ability to learn was related to the social environment.

Since then, of course, numerous studies have found similar results. Yet, anthropologists and many others have held onto the idea that genes are more important than the environment. People like Arthur Jensen in the 60s and 1970s argued that intelligence was 85% genes, while Murray and Herrenstein in the *Bell Curve* echoed his work. They argued that genes were the reason for all group differences including class differences. Most of the studies cited in the *Bell Curve* were old and had been debunked decades ago. For instance, they treated correlations in IQ scores between parent and offspring for occupation as genetically based when, of course if my dad was a dentist it is likely that I would become a dentist. As a matter of fact, as a teenager I may already know how to pull a tooth and understand dental terminology so of course I will score high on a test related to dentistry. This does not mean, as they would argue, that I carry genes for becoming a dentist. They completely ignored learning, and treated social transmission of, for instance, study habits, as if it was a part of biological transmission. A correlation represents an association, not a cause and effect!

For some anthropologists, social factors confounded their genetic model. They tried to standardize or reduce the effect of social factors by making them equal, while the trait they pursued varied. For example, when looking at low-birth weight infants and infant mortality, Black infant mortality exceeds that for Whites in each category of socioeconomic status (SES). Also, the highest SES Blacks have more infant mortality than the lowest SES Whites. Blacks in the same SES as Whites have higher infant mortality. These results have been taken to prove that Blacks have a genetic predisposition toward infant mortality. But SES does not capture a lifetime of health problems, and while SES status may have changed, individuals and populations were still burdened by a lifetime of exposure to environmental insult (Geronimus, 1992, 1996). In other words, just because Blacks and Whites were in the same SES did not mean that they were comparable. Blacks had a life before they were in that SES where they were most likely subjected to poor health care, under nutrition, and exposure to infectious as well as toxic environments.

Toddler

One of my professors at the University of Alabama was Mr. DeJarnette. We were all warned not to mess with him. I didn't know what that meant until I took his class. If you asked what he considered to be a dumb question, he threw an eraser or piece of chalk at you. Not one to waste time on foolishness, he came to teach archaeology and expected you to learn it. On a dig at Moundville, he fired one of the student supervisors eight times in one day!

Still, it wasn't all bad as we used to party at Moundville. There were always a number of kegs of beer and plenty of food. Anthropologists, I came to learn, live for those two things. After people were fully inebriated we would look for a bird whose name I've since forgotten, that supposedly lives at Moundville. But you could only catch it in a brown paper bag. So there would be all of these people running around the mounds yelling out a bird citing and people would run to that spot with their paper bags trying to catch this bird.

Colombia, South America

During the summer of 1973, we went to Colombia, South America where I completed a six-hour course in ethnographic field methods with Dr. C. Earle Smith, an ethnobotanist. Three students participated and we were to collect data on some topic that had been pre-approved. Becky did a study on household structure, while I did mine on fingerprints. I don't know what Chip's project was supposed to have been, but it was clear from the beginning that he just wanted to go to Colombia. As a matter of fact he left us after Villavencia and went to Carracus.

I looked at the prevalence of different types of fingerprint patterns (there are three basic kinds — whorls, loops, and arches) and number of ridges to see how the population in the villages that we visited compared to populations in other parts of the world. I did it the old fashion way with them dipping their fingers in an ink pad and then rolling their finger onto paper.

When we arrived in Bogotá, Dr. Smith already had our hotel arranged and he knew a lot of people from his previous visits. It was a new experience for me with all of the urchins (begging children) around us all the time. Knowing that we were Americans they assumed we had money to give and would follow us. Bogotá is a large city but it was not uncommon to see people carrying huge bundles of hay on their head or back or pulling wooden wagons with wood wheels. We stayed in Bogotá for a couple of days where we shopped; I bought some beautiful jade that was really inexpensive.

We went to a small village Inirida where we stayed for a week. It was really the jungle. At night we heard wild animals like tigers and lepers in the jungle. One night we decided to sit by the river and Dr. Smith told us that wasn't such a good idea since animals might want to drink water there. There was no running water in the village and no electricity. We slept on cots that really made you ache all over. During the day women washed at the river, people drank from and also excreted in it. We drank bottled water and hot beer. I had already taken some Spanish classes but I wasn't fluent by any means as I went door to door to tell people about the study. They were very willing to participate. I don't recall anyone refusing. The kids really loved to get ink on their hands. My Spanish did get better as I talked to them about the study and who lived in the house. I did that most of the day for about a week.

We had a cook who cooked eggs for us for breakfast, lunch, and dinner. In some way she managed to boil or fry an egg and make it part of the meal. Sometimes she would lay a sunny-side up egg over soup. It would be soup with potatoes or some type of meat. I don't know what it was. We had chicken (the wild type that's tough). During the day we would see chickens walking around the village and we knew that one of them would be on our table that evening. It was so hot whenever we got a meal we were really hungry. It made you eat whatever they put in front of you.

One of Dr. Smith's friends had a finca (farm) a few miles from the village. His friend's son, Jeff, came to the village to take us to visit the finca, which turned out to be quite an adventure. Wearing mud boots (the name said it all, even though they were nothing more than tough, rubber rain boots) we had to trek through the jungles, cutting branches with our machetes. We tried to cross a creek that was covered with numerous large boulders. I slipped, fell into a hole in one of the large rocks, and went completely under. There was no room to try to swim because the opening in the rock was small, just enough for my body to slip into, but not large enough for me to move my arms. Fortunately, I hit the bottom and pushed up with my feet. I bobbed up like a floater and they grabbed me when I came up. Then the fear of my experience really hit me, realizing that if I had gone down again, coming back up wasn't a certainty.

We were treated to a really nice dinner when we arrived at the finca. Although there was no ice to cool us from the heat of our travels, dinner consisted of lapa, a cross between a rabbit and a rat. It was good, but I didn't want the part with the claw. Hot water was another luxury, leaving a cold shower as the only option there was no place to wash up in the village except in the river. We stayed there that night and the next day returned to the village with his son.

While we came to the village in a Cessna (that was quite an experience flying over mountains in such a small plane) we left on a cargo plane. The seats were placed along the sides of the plane and were more like benches. In addition to us, the plane carried chickens, goats and pigs. While flying we would have to put one foot on a pig and maybe another foot on a goat to keep them off of us. The flight was over an hour so it was pretty rough. As we moved from one village to another, we submitted to searches by the police for contraband. That too was kind of scary for there was no trusting that they wouldn't plant anything on an American that could land you in jail. In countries like Colombia you could get twenty years for one marijuana cigarette.

Villavencia, also called Villavo was a beautiful small town. The entire environment reminded me of early confrontations between the invading conquistadors and the indigenous natives' futile attempts to defend their land. Spanish influence has remained evident, especially in the large haciendas. It was a magnificent place with beautiful sunsets, large mango trees, palm trees and an assortment of colorful birds flying around. Here, thank goodness, we could get cold beer. We ate lots of chicken and fish. The fish was whole with the eyes on it. It was delicious but I would put some bread over the head because I couldn't bear to stare in dead fish eyes as I was eating.

While we were in Villavo, Dr. Smith's friend, Ben (Jeff's father) came for us in his jeep. Ben had really gone native, living like a swashbuckler. As he drove the jeep around winding curves over steep cliffs, he drank whiskey and talked. We were concerned with him drinking and driving in such a treacherous environment. Every now and then Dr. Smith would look back at us and smile. He knew we were afraid, but I think he saw this cliffhanger experience as a way for us to be baptized into the field. Anthropologists often talk about what terrible thing happened to them while they were in the field, bitten by snakes, assaulted by parasites, or contracting some exotic illness like malaria. Once you start fieldwork everyone has a story to tell, and I've collected my share over the years.

Well we finally reached his hacienda and enjoyed a really nice meal. It was a large place. As expected, there was no air conditioning, but the top of the opened wall allowed air to circulate. It was wonderful to look at the mountains outside my window.

Returning to Villavo, we went to another small village not too far away where I continued collecting fingerprints. We met an English couple that wanted to get a feel for Colombia outside of the touristy area, even though they stayed in the same village where they had cabins. We took a boat ride on the Orinoco River, another dangerous adventure because the whirlpools in the river had to be carefully navigated. We sometimes saw animals like monkeys along the coastline.

We met many local people, outside of the data collection. At night we would sit around, drinking beer and talking about our lives with one another. You really got to know people, especially after a few beers.

Other Field Work

My senior year, Ken Turner joined the faculty and my life changed. Inexplicably, the red-haired White man took me under his wings and decided to make me into an anthropologist. I loved my courses with him. It was then that I took becoming an anthropologist seriously. Instead of partying in the evening, I began working in the lab with his bone collection. The university had a large collection of Native American Indians skeletal material that dated back 2,000 years. Working with Ken, I learned what to look for, for instance, to determine sex, not hard when you know what to look for and after you've seen a lot of skeletons. Determining pathologies promised more difficulty, but again, the ones that left their mark on bones such as iron deficiency and some infections have a particular pattern and appearance. This was my heyday for bone work. Sometimes Ken would stop me in the hallway and hand me a bone. I would have to identify it without looking.

I collected data for my thesis at the Ramsey Building that housed the Native American skeletal collection for Moundville. It was an old building with electricity but no heating. All of the burials were in barrel-like containers. Many of them had not been examined for years. Since there was no heat I had to wear a coat and I wore gloves with the fingers cut out so I could take measurements. Pushing a little cart down the aisle, I measured one burial after another. It was kind of scary because I found snake skins in some of them, which made me paranoid to the idea of reaching in and touching a snake.

I was there for about three months, from sun up (7 a.m.) to sun down (late at night). Since I was bundled up inside there was no way to know what was happening outside. One day it rained so hard that when I came out that night I was stuck in the mud. I began crying because I didn't want to stay out there with those Indians. I panicked for a while, running around in circles before remembering that a caretaker lived on the grounds. But I would have to go through some mounds to find him and I didn't relish that. Fortunately, he came down the road before I'd gone too far and used his tractor to pull me out. I decided it might not be such a good idea to stay there so late.

Once they found a skeleton north of the university and we went out to remove it. That was an exciting experience because I learned how to excavate a burial, both a complicated and extremely time consuming task. We couldn't go in with a backhoe and destroy it. We used dental tools to meticulously remove the hard dirt and a camel-hair brush to remove the debris. Next, we covered it with tissue paper and applied shellac so that it didn't fall apart. Applying a plaster of paris, we let it dry before we removed the entire skeleton and cleaned it at the lab.

We went into one of the caves where you could still find arrow points and it was like air conditioning. Native Americans lived in beautiful surroundings. They didn't need to build elaborate structures as they lived where nature already created such surroundings.

Since there wasn't a medical examiner in the immediate vicinity, Ken sometimes got bones that needed to be examined to determine age, sex, and to personally identify the individual. It was not as romantic as the movie series "Crime Scene Investigators (CSI)" Once we received a body in a suitcase that came from somewhere in Wisconsin. The bones were a bright White because they poured Clorox on them. It was apparent what killed the woman, a bullet wound in the head. Through forensics techniques we were able to age, sex, and race the individual. That was an eye opener for me and showed me another side of anthropology.

I began my work in anthropology as an osteologist where I studied bones. My initial work was on Native American Indians. The title of my thesis was *A Study of Biological Relationships Between Archaic and Mississippian Skeletal Populations in Northern Alabama*, 1979. The archaic period was between 8000-1000 BC and the Mississippian from 1000-1350 ad. I tried to determine if you could place post-cranial skeletal into one of these time periods based upon physical differences in limb bones. I assumed that differences would be due to cultural factors such as subsistence patterns. What I was being taught was how to categorize people into boxes. I learned to make race real. That people could be placed into boxes because they had certain characteristics.

While examining hundreds of skeletons housed at Moundville State Park, I observed pathologies on the bones. Bones exhibited pathologies such as osteoarthritis, osteoporosis, periostitis, osteomyelitis and other infections. In addition, some had fractures that had healed badly. They also suffered from porotic hyperostosis, iron deficiency and vitamin D deficiency which causes the legs to bow.

The University of Alabama provided an enjoyable time as well as a good learning experience for me. I basically had a tutor, Dr. Turner, who really cared about my welfare and wanted me to get a doctorate (Alabama only has a master's in anthropology). When I planned to take a job one summer to pay my bills he let me teach a course that he was scheduled to teach so I could have money and work on my thesis. That too was a learning experience because I had never taught a course before. He gave me examples of his syllabus. Many of the professors there gave me advice. Dr. Smith said," Remember, you know more than them." Dr. Richard Krause said, "Just think of them as cabbages." Looking out at the students on my first day of class all I could see were rows of cabbages.

Genes: Is That All There Is?

In 1978 I went to the University of Kansas to study under Dr. Michael Crawford. He had also been Ken's professor when he attended graduate school there. I was considered the granddaughter. We worked on the genetics of baboons where we looked at their pedigrees to determine possible genetic transmission of leukemia among them, examined fingerprints from Ireland by examining their pedigrees to determine genetic relationships, and studied aging among the Mennonites in Goessel, Kansas.

It was believed that Mennonites live longer than other people. (By this time, I had begun to wear glasses, probably from counting ridges on fingerprints.) We looked at chronological versus biological aging among the Mennonites, using physiological methods such as hand-eye coordination. We took all kinds of tests such as weight, height, vision, as well as PTC (Phenylthiocarbamide, a human-made chemical similar to one found in nature). It was believed that the ability to taste this chemical could, for instance, help individuals avoid foods that produced goiters and hypothyroidism in low-iodine environments. On one occasion, I dispensed PTC from extremely high concentrations to extremely low concentrations in a circle so it wouldn't appear that there was a ranking. I forgot which end was which so I had to test it. And believe me, this was some nasty stuff (tasted poisonous like Clorox or ammonia)! But the Mennonites were extremely nice and needless to say, patient, always polite and willing to do whatever we wanted. They would wait all day until we called them to say take body measurements. Then they would sit somewhere until we called them to draw blood and then sit again until we called them to do something else. It was a joy working with them. After all the testing-abuse we heaped on them, they were gracious enough to even cook for us. They made their own sausage, and bread called zweebog that was absolutely delicious.

Around 1982, I began the search for a dissertation topic. Having worked on Mennonites, I considered doing something on aging but the data wasn't inclusive enough. Additional variables were needed to have a good hypothesis and since returning to the community to collect more data was problematic due to lack of funding I dropped that topic. It was then that I stumbled across hypertension in the literature while conducting a search for one of my professors on another topic. (We didn't have the Internet to do searches; you had to thumb through dusty, old journals.) After going through a multitude of abstracts and articles, I ran across an interesting piece by George Comstock entitled *An Epidemiological Study of Blood Pressure Levels in a Biracial Community in the Southern U.S.* The high mortality of hypertension among African Americans alarmed me. He showed higher blood pressures among Blacks than Whites after the age of 25 years. Then I began to read articles about blood pressure among Africans such as Kaminer and Lutz's *Blood Pressure in Bushmen of the Kalahari Desert* (1960) and Williams' *Blood Pressure Differences in Kikuyu and Samburu Communities in Kenya* (1969).

I realized that while African Americans showed an increase in blood pressure with age, this was not true in rural African societies where there was a gradual elevation in blood pressure with increasing age compared to a rapid increase with age among African Americans. Also, the prevalence of hypertension in rural African groups was low, less than 10% until they moved to urban areas where it increased (Kaminer and Lutz, 1960). For African Americans the prevalence was 20-30%. West Indians such as Jamaicans had higher pressures in urban than rural areas. Also, unlike Africans, Black West Indians showed noticeable increases in blood pressure level with advancing age. It was apparent that social issues influenced blood pressure. It was not just genetics.

Assuming genetics was the reason for the elevated blood pressure, pedigrees and correlated blood pressures among genetically related individuals were drawn up. Path analysis was used to examine the transmissibility of traits by calculating correlations between standardized variables (to eliminate the effects of age, weight, etc and get at only the 'genetic'). While these techniques sounded good, I didn't think they separated the genetic from the family environment. In other words, the reason for similarity in blood pressure between parent and adult offspring may not be genetics but attributable to similar diet and other types of social environment. I ended up writing a dissertation entitled: *A Biocultural Analysis of Blood Pressure Variation among the Black Caribs and Creoles of St. Vincent, West Indies.*

As a graduate student I learned how a lifestyle of hard manual work affected the body and reduced lifespan. More importantly, I realized that a lot of the diseases in the Black community could be prevented if people had access to health insurance and physicians that they felt comfortable with. When I was growing up, bowlegs were not only common, but it was considered cute. Kwashiorkor (insufficient protein where the stomach is swollen and the individual looks fat but they're not) has rarely been seen today, although it can be found in poor neighborhoods. However, getting enough food was not and is not the only issue Black people in Birmingham faced. They were sickly because they worked in steel mills at hard jobs everyday and received very little medical care.

Many Black people did not want to go to the doctor because they did not want to deal with White people. Instead, they would stay at home and try their own remedies. Sometimes, this could kill us too. My father was a nurse's aid in a hospital and he talked about how Blacks were treated differently from the White ones. Not only did they have to wait longer for service, the doctors assumed that they wouldn't follow the regimen so they did not give them the same dosage or prescriptions.

In my studies at Kansas, genetics were stressed to explain all differences. This smacked of the racism that I experienced while growing up which attributed occupational attainment as well as health to Black biological constitution. In other words, Blacks were in low paying jobs because they were not capable of skilled or intellectual-oriented positions. High disease rates were due to biology and not living conditions caused by segregation, unequal access to resources and poor health care.

But, biological differences between racial groups have accounted for a small difference in disease between racial groups. Richard Cooper demonstrated that of the thousands of excess Black deaths in 1977, only 0.3% was attributed to diseases such as sickle cell. No evidence, however, linked susceptibility to disease as falling along racial lines (Cooper and David, 1986). Nevertheless, such diseases were used to support genetic explanations of racial variation in twentieth century diseases such as cancer, stroke and heart disease. Again, there has been no evidence to justify such extrapolation (Krieger and Bassett, 1986). Genes ... "are almost always a minor, unstable, and insufficient cause" of disease (Goodman, 2000:1700). Genes have not been shown to be a major cause of differences in disease and death rates between populations (races), but physical anthropologists have continued talking about it as if they do.

Studies also showed that the differences in stress level affected blood pressure because of the type of society we live in. That was why African Americans have had such high blood pressure (another can be attributed to diet). Part of the stress could be blamed on racism in society, which was not an issue in rural African societies and less so in the Caribbean. Body fat, exercise, diet, stress have also been contributing factors in explaining blood pressure differences.

By 1983, I was a visiting Professor at Wichita State University. I accepted a teaching position so I could earn enough money to support myself while I finished my doctorate. I ached to leave Kansas! When you work on something like a dissertation you sort of lose site of life and the degree becomes the life. It was a type of madness unrealized until it's over. I was really insane at that time, but that was the norm for a graduate student.

Coming from an academic background at Kansas that stressed genetics, I published a number of articles on the genetics of hypertension. (*The Relationship Between African Admixture and Blood Pressure Variation in the Caribbean, Human Heredity*, 36:12-18, 1986; *Genetic Determinants of Blood Pressure Levels among the Black Caribs of St. Vincent, Human Biology*, 53: 453-66, 1981, to name a few.) You have to keep in mind that we started out with a genetic model and looked for an association between some physiological characteristic and a disease such as hypertension. Anything else was played down because the title of the article would lead you to the conclusion.

Of course growing up in the south, I knew that the reason for our diseases and low-level jobs were thought to be our genetic inferiority. I always had a problem with looking at something as totally the result of genetics. Keep in mind though that many physical anthropologists were and still are genetically oriented.

Outward physical differences make it seem that we are fundamentally different. However, the Human Genome Project has shown just the opposite. There is only a 1% genetic difference between what we call races. Considering the millions of bases, nucleic acid, on the chromosome, 1% is negligible. Because of the outward differences, people, including scientists, forget that we have 99% genetic similarity. Even the outward differences are due not only to genes but also to environmental factors. For instance, you have tall linear people in hot climates because it increases the surface area for sweating. Over time, natural selection selected for individuals with this characteristic. In other words, since they could sweat more efficiently, the sweat evaporates and cools the skin, these individuals had a better chance of surviving in a hot climate. Populations did not evolve separately. Rather they adapted to differing environments. However, there was always intermixture so no population went on its own evolutionary journey. Through gene flow populations were always pulled back or connected to the species. As a result, all people can interbreed with one another and produce offspring who can do the same thing.

However, what we know to be true about humankind in general remains a "but" when the information is applied to African Americans, with a racist restructuring which supports that even if humankind evolved from common ancestors, as Darwinism proposed, Whites and Blacks evolved so differently as to make the point moot (Nobles, 2000). As I throw up my hands in frustration sometimes, I can but restate the proven: We are one species. We all have forty-six chromosomes.

Chapter Nine

What Price A Degree?

"It seems like I've witnessed more racism than anybody."

It was while in Wichita that I happened across a job advertisement from the Anthropology Department at the University of Houston. They were looking for a physical anthropology professor who was also a medical anthropologist. The job description read as if it had been written for me. It wasn't long before I realized that it was, and it wasn't.

Overcoming the legacy of discrimination has all but been abandoned in the argument supporting affirmative action. Diversity has become the new code word, considered important by educators today to create a learning environment in which all students are prepared to live and work together with people of all races (Bowen and Bok, 1998). However, the belief that diversity as a worthy and constitutional goal for institutions of higher education was supported as early as 1954 in Brown v. Board of Education (Wohl, 2001). The focus then, though, was overcoming the legacy of discrimination. Today, the goal of diversity is to create an enriched learning environment through exposure to diverse perspectives and approaches to problems. Diversity is to enrich the education of students and not to provide equal opportunity for people of color.

Universities have been content to showcase the number of minorities they have because it suggests that they are progressive and inclusive, additionally serving as a public relations device with minority communities and in the recruitment of minority students. But the academic community has not been receptive to the inclusion of knowledge and ways of thinking by minority academics. The gift of knowledge and insight they could bestow has not been incorporated into the discipline, only minority bodies to show that the department is diverse (Alvarez, 1994).

At the University of Houston, there were 24 Black professors on the payroll out of a faculty of close to 1,000 when I arrived there in 1984. The numbers are the same in 2005. The student body, however, has changed currently being: 13.2% Black, 18.6% Asian, 17.8% Hispanic, 8% International, 39.8% White, and 2.2% other. While administration recognized that a more diverse faculty was needed, they seemed unwilling to do what was necessary to bring about an increase in Black faculty on campus. Departments were unwilling to actively seek Black faculty because they wanted "the best person for the position." Accordingly, race should not matter, however race and racism are largely the reasons that they and their predecessors got their initial job. It continues with departments hiring friends and those like themselves.

Recruitment of minorities at predominantly White universities has been symbolic of fulfilling institutional goals and requirements to diversify the faculty population. The operative word has been symbolic as Robert Alvarez discovered. In efforts to recruit minorities, universities operate in "...secrecy, manipulation, misused power, and reasserted hierarchy" (1994:260).

In an interview process at an Ivy League school, a colleague recounted how a Hispanic faced intense grilling from morning to night at an interview and then was asked to come back for a follow-up interview. In that same department, they hired a White male without an interview because everyone knew him. When this was pointed out to one of the professors in the department, his jaw almost dropped to the floor. He admitted there had been biased and seemed astonished when he began to deal with it.

Along that same vein, Alvarez experienced an effort to recruit him, but not to hire him. Some cited that the position should be available to all candidates and not just minorities (ignoring biases due to the "good old boy" system) while others contended that they already had one Chicano in their department and saw no need to hire another one.

However, the recruitment of minorities into anthropology has not resulted in the inclusion of new perspectives and knowledge from such persons. Minorities have really been little more than public relations spokespersons hired to perform as intermediaries between White administrators who are uncomfortable dealing with minority communities. Similarly, programs such as African American Studies and Mexican American Studies when blessed as a component of the university have been instituted to serve as public relations offices, expected to deal with minority issues and report back to the administration.

My interview at the University of Houston went well, and the job became mine. I arrived on the campus of the University of Houston in 1984. Not long afterward, I learned that I was hired through the minority program. There was absolutely no mention whatsoever in the advertisement that a "minority" was being sought to fill the position. And no one wanted to tell me! Fortuitously, I learned from Black professors that all minority hires were through that program. Anger doesn't begin to describe how I felt. I was immensely qualified for the job and no explanation satisfied my understanding as to why I had to be hired through a special program.

The way this worked was that most of the salary was paid by the university at the beginning, and over the years the amount the university pays is reduced while the college becomes responsible for the bulk of the expenses. This was allegedly designed to encourage colleges within the university to hire minorities. Actually, what it did was to make you and your colleagues feel as if you received something that you would not have received otherwise — even if you were qualified. Since most medical anthropologists have traditionally been cultural anthropologists, many people would not have been qualified to apply for that job (a medical/physical anthropologist).

I was among the few—Black, White, yellow, or polka dot—who met the specifications of the job description. Yet, I was treated as a special case, with the implications that I lacked the necessary qualifications for the job. Even knowing I have not been the only one this has happened to, the practice has continued to piss me off.

During my stay at the university, I have felt this pattern of special case on a continual basis. This branding (another form of labeling that suggest unfit, and a whole bunch of other negative connotations) has largely been attributed to the needs of the university, not to my needs or the needs of minorities. We have been put on all kinds of committees for show only. In true science fiction fashion, we were to de-cloak: lend your name, show up to meetings to prove your *minorityness*, but be quiet, bury your expertise, and keep your ideas to yourself. And when they're done with you, you were expected to return to cloak status. ("Scottie, beam me up cause there's no intelligent life on earth," as Gil Scott-Heron lamented.)

Departments at my university have demonstrated disinterest in actively pursuing minorities, using the excuse that they won't be able to hire someone that they "want" in the future. Under the context of wanting to hire the best person hides the truth. This so-called 'best' person refers to hiring someone who looks like the majority population. However, to show their largesse, they have requested among the few members of the Black faculty to submit resumes of prospective faculty; thus implying that a Black person is better qualified to spot quality in another Black person. I have submitted twelve 'qualified' individuals, ranging from chemistry and biology to English and political science. All of the proper procedures and channels were adhered to, but it was all a sham as no one has attempted to recruit any of the people even though they would not have required tenure immediately. The candidate would have at least five years to determine if they should be tenured. Although it could be argued that departments do not want to consider candidates that are not generated from within their departments. The fact remains, however, that no one was even willing to consider any of the candidates, leading to only one obvious conclusion.

If I expected better from my colleagues, shame on me. Rather than a demonstration of broadmindedness or even a phony face, there have been repeated overt attempts to prevent the university from hiring Black faculty. Even when administrators became aware of such deceitful strategy, they responded with little more than a facade of recruiting. It was fighting against the odds. White faculty believed that an attempt to recruit Black scholars was doing something special for them, failing to see their recruitment of mediocre friends as special.

Our parents taught us, which was then reinforced by the system that a Black person had to be an exceptional academic to be hired. Mediocrity was a qualification reserved for Whites only. A colleague recounted a situation in his department where a White male was hired without the faculty even reviewing his resume. It was tacitly assumed that he was a good scholar. Yet, on a different occasion, a Black man was being considered and not only did they want his vitae, but he had to give a number of guest lectures on campus, spend a lot of time with each faculty, and then return for a second visit. He was not selected.

This White academic culture has been cemented and will not change unless forced. Departments have tipped their hands, showing they have not been committed to diversity, insuring that they will remain Lilly White. The response of administration hasn't changed either, evident through their lack of action. After undergoing a push to get minorities and women, claiming to want diversity, they would rather work the few already employed to death than hire new faculty. Not only a sore spot, but also this practice has escalated into a major problem, leading to burnout among Black scholars, the educationally emaciated whose hope straddles the fence.

With insights ignored juxtaposed to committee assignments that are tantamount to busy work, there is little denying that Black scholars are devalued. Naturally, the exceptions do exist, but by-and-large, we are forced to fight the same old battles year-in and year-out, around the clock because we have remained hopeful that a change will come and that in some way we can make a significant contribution toward such a revolution. But this frustration is not limited to the halls of academia.

When I graduated, well even before then, I attended national meetings of the American Association of Physical Anthropologists, American Anthropological Association and some smaller conferences. I was always eager to go to the meetings to meet people, network and learn about their work, as well as share my work through a number of presentations. After a decade or so disenchantment cast a pall cloud over these affairs. After about six or seven years, it was clear that the same people presented over and over again, giving the same talk, like a song in-the-round. One guy even used the same slides from one year to the next. If the professor wasn't giving the same talk, then his student was giving the same talk that he gave the previous year. Nothing new was offered, but it wasn't that nothing new had been developed.

People of color often had a different approach, but were not taken seriously. Yet, a White person, the following year, could make the same statement and it is something new, (i.e., postmodernism where you deconstruct text). We have been doing this since day one. W.E.B. DuBois and St. Claire Drake, for instance, were postmodernists, but their work was trapped on the sidelines of mainstream academia and consequently ignored. When a White person came along and talked about looking at something a new way and gave it a name, then there was a "paradigm shift." This theft represented a continual cooptation of work by people of color without giving them credit. They often spoke about social capital, but herein again, DuBois discussed it in the early 1920s. Not only did the White scholars in his day fail to credit him, he has not been given credit for his valuable work today.

Even in hindsight, I am positive that this situation went beyond a hurt of crushed egos. Tragically, the intellectual "dissing" from our national peers mimicked that which we received back in our university homes. As anthropologists, I expected broader perspectives, an open-mindedness different from what had been exhibited by my university colleagues. In my naiveté, I failed to remember that they were products of the racist environments they came from. Now, I know why I stopped seeing some people at the meetings that I used to see on a regular basis: they got burned out and so did I.

Aside from long-time Black activists who scratched and clawed for equality, anthropologists know more than most about the hazards of racism. As a whole, however, this learned field of scholars has been unwilling to act on their knowledge for change when knowledge requires action. St. Claire Drake, another Black anthropologist whose invaluable contributions on the study of race have gone ignored, formulated this position to which I subscribe. He believed that while revealing the social construction of race and racism and its many ramifications on society was good, one also needed to take direct action to destroy racist beliefs and behaviors. As you might imagine, this went against Eurocentric standards of scholarship, whereby, one is to be outside of the subject so as to be "objective," in plain denial of human capability.

While detachment is a requirement in academia to be a scholar, there is no such thing as objectivity. St. Claire Drake drew on Mannheim's system of knowledge, arguing that culture is embedded in knowledge. Knowledge is not separate from what we bring to the table—our belief system and values at home. (We hope one never leaves home without them.) We then intertwine our cultural experience with data to produce knowledge. Everyone brings baggage to the table, a natural human phenomenon. As racism is inherently a part of the belief system in American society, it too, impacts knowledge. In spite of our knowledge, objectivity and passivity are academic standards that many academics, Black and White alike, adhere to.

But many Black anthropologists are attracted to this discipline because the analysis provided by Drake has the power to liberate Black people from racism. In other words, we can "out" racism, make it bare and naked so that the world could witness the impact it has upon them as individuals, as well as on the structure of their societies. Unfortunately, because Drake focused on liberating Black people through exposing racism, his work was considered peripheral, nonscientific, not objective, and unscholarly. His *Black Metropolis* (1945), a classic work in urban anthropology, went unheralded until 1988 when Faye V.

Harrison appraised it in "Introduction: An African Diaspora Perspective for Urban Anthropology."

The book received harsh criticism by leading anthropologists who accused the authors, Drake and Cayton, of misinterpreting the data in which they argued that a fluid casteless system explained the data as opposed to a status caste system. Drake and Cayton included Black Nationalism and Marxism in their analysis of the Black community in Chicago, revealing how racism has been used systematically to privilege Whites, the financial beneficiaries of such injustice.

White anthropology, on the other hand, was enmeshed with British structural functionalism and Parkian sociology of race relations. This lack of visibility for such a notable work exemplifies the peripheralization of Black scholars in anthropology. Whenever Black scholars combine race and racism with economics, their works have not only been questioned and challenged as a normal discourse of criticism, but also discredited and disqualified as not worthy of public dissemination. This means that such views are not likely to be published in "mainstream" journals. It is institutional racism in academia that intensifies when racism is "outed". Rather than deal with the truth and accept racism for what it is and what it has done, we've had a new term introduced into the fold to replace an aspect of institutional racism, euphemistically called "environmental justice[1]." (But if it looks like a duck, and quacks like a duck, then ...)

To be an African American and anthropologist who is Black-centered does not mean that data will be modified to out racism. Black-centered anthropologists are just as objective as other anthropologists who do not formally acknowledge their centeredness. I am not afraid to do so. That does not mean that my research lacks scholarship, but that I am aware of the origin of my hypotheses. It does not mean that the scientific method of data collection will be altered. It means that a broad variety of data will be collected. It does not mean that the analysis will be biased, but that a variety of theoretical orientations will be examined to determine what fits the data. There is no agenda: there is only a subject.

Fighting on another front, it is incumbent upon Black scholars to keep Black students in school when the university doesn't care if they're there or not. We also have to publish on topics that Whites feel are appropriate and cite people in our work that are acceptable to them, or our papers will not be published in mainstream journals; therefore, we will not get tenure. We have to fight being on committee after committee because the university wants a person of color on it, although it does not count in terms of getting tenure. As a result, we have to spend time doing things that won't help us to keep our job, yet they want to know why we aren't as prolific as our White colleagues. Then of course there is the basic form of disrespect we must contend with from racist colleagues who think that we can only talk about issues related to Black people. I have pretty much stopped talking to one colleague because over a ten-year period he never discussed anything with me that was not related to Black people as if I had no other interests.

As a practitioner of my discipline as well as a teaching professor, it has seemed that I've witnessed more racism than anybody. I didn't know what I was getting into by pursuing a career in anthropology, and sometimes, I still don't know. Nevertheless, when I entered college, I knew that I wanted to major in anthropology. Since the beginning of my training as an anthropologist, I have tried to understand human variation, both culturally and biologically. There was no attempt to disprove traditional or standard thinking about variation, but to provide a perspective devoid of racist overtones. This was not a vindication approach to correct distorted versions about minorities as espoused by St. Claire Drake. Nor, was there a sacrificing of objectivity in anthropological research. Like other social scientists, I drew on a variety of data and tried to explain the phenomena by using the most likely explanation. Often, I used a postmodernist approach to sort out contemporary understandings and reframe them in a way that revealed their relationships.

While many of my White colleagues may have been unconcerned about the particular population that they study, I have focused on minorities, especially African Americans. This life work was related to my ancestry, for sure, but it does not control my approach to studying my group. Rather, it provided access to individuals toward gaining a fuller knowledge of what it means to be Black in the world today. I am one Black person and I never assumed that I understood things because I am Black. Rather, I have probed and prodded, providing individuals the opportunity to discuss their perspectives without my own assumptions. Therein rested an objectivity coupled with connections to populations that allowed the potential for such connections, and an ease of communication that might not have been as forthright between people of differing ethnicities. Studying Black people has meant using standard anthropological methods. But that has also included allowing the interviewees to identify with the interviewer.

When I received my PhD in anthropology I quickly learned that the degree was not just mine. There were numerous needs within the Black community, and as Black scholars, we must share in those concerns. It is not enough that we just work in the ivory tower and ignore the services and/or contributions we can make to the community as in some ways it is because of the community that we are at the university, figureheads or not. As soon as I arrived on campus at UH, somehow, people in the Black community discovered that I was there and called me about all types of issues, concerns, information, and research that they needed done. Issues ranged from trying to document the historic nature of abandoned Black cemeteries to speaking on domestic violence or the civil rights movement. People often wanted information about a variety of things. For instance, one woman from the Cameroon wanted to know how to go about getting asylum in the United States. She had slipped out of the country with her children without permission from her husband (in Africa the children belong to the husband) and she did not want to return. Others wanted information about study skills for their children, a speaker on Black vernacular, or someone to teach prisoners basic reading skills. Often, I was the unofficial librarian, a facilitator for and of information. Surprisingly, oftentimes I knew just the person(s) to contact to get the information that they wanted.

This connection to the community was often symbolic, as well. When people, even my seniors, would call me Doctor, I would often invite them to call me Janis. But they insisted on using the title, Doctor or Doc. One day I asked a friend why he kept calling me doctor and he explained that he liked calling me that. He liked the fact that I hold a PhD. The sense of pride this instills explains in part why I stay and do battle, having been touched by the realization that when I got my degree, it was for the community, too. When I earned that PhD, the Black community also got a PhD.

Chapter Ten

Other Worlds

"Life Experiences as Field Experiences"

I have never gotten over my fondness for field trips that began in elementary school. I'm not going to say they have more meaning now, but they definitely mean more than the respite from bomb scars that they used to hold. Field studies provide an opportunity to touch. Data collection represents a necessary tool in the quest for answers to problems, or to understand more intrinsically than a surface view could provide the hows, whys, and impact things, tangible and non-tangible, have on our way of living by collecting data.

Even though the conclusions drawn by African Americans have continued to be unacknowledged or outright rejected by mainstream scientists of the anthropological family, it does not negate the necessity of conducting field studies, findings, or the interpretation of the data. Historically, Blacks have not been studied unless it was to deny that people of African ancestry ever did anything of significance. Either we were portrayed as never having contributed to civilization, or our culture and way of life were devalued and made less than significant. Studying one's culture does not suggest a lack of objectivity, rather, it offers a holistic view.

Being an African American is broader than the world of Americans and broader than the world of Africans. It is something bigger than that because reality is more complex than imposed boundaries. African Americans are combinations of cultural elements and viewpoints that created something broader than being an African in America or an American African. There is enormous variation in this population in terms of not only behavior but also cultural orientation, way of life and not to forget class differences and educational and religious variation. What I study is variation in this scenario. Therefore, I study the *other* in the African Diaspora while simultaneously being the *other*.

While in college, field studies offered more than an opportunity not only to bolster my experience, but relief from the humdrum of spending summers in Kansas. Since that time, they have helped in cementing my professionally philosophy and personal beliefs. I'll never forget that it felt like a reward when I got to experience the impact of a less-stressful social environment, making two separate trips to St, Vincent in 1982 and 1983. My first time was with Dr. Michael Crawford and Dr. Paul Lin, a Taiwanese ex-patriot. Since Dr. Crawford had been there before we already had hotel and travel arrangements.

We were studying the Black Caribs or Garifuna who were a mixture of Arawak Indian and African slave ancestry. They lived in the northern part of the island where we traveled on a daily basis. The bus that was supposed to go north each day often broke down so we hired someone or thumbed a ride on the back of a truck. In Sandy Bay and Owia, we worked with the nurse at the clinic, taking body measurements, fingerprints again, and drew blood for genetic studies. I collected information on households so we could draw pedigrees.

At night we would return to the city where we had rooms with no air conditioning, but there was always a breeze. The cook made chicken or fish every night. Vegetables were hard to come by; beef likewise was a rarity, but we ate a lot of yucca and plantains. After dinner we would sit around and talk and drink cold beer.

You really got to know people from these discussions. Paul was torn between his love for Taiwan but wanting to live in America. For most people, that was hard to understand for he had lived in the United States for over thirty years. Listening to him, I remembered thinking that he retained his accent to hold onto his Taiwanese ancestry as a form of resistance to assimilation. Mike Crawford was from a family of Russian refugees. They lived in a refugee camp in the Philippines and eventually moved to the United States. When they arrived here his dad, who was an Engineer in Russia, could only find a job as a clerk. It was hard for them growing up in poverty; sometimes people wouldn't rent to them because of their accent. Today, he has no accent, not even a regional one. He empathized with me, I believe, because he and his family had been subjected to discrimination.

I returned to St. Vincent the following summer alone. On the way, I stopped in Barbados but my luggage went to Port of Prince. I learned something about traveling then: always carry enough for overnight in a bag on the plane with you. I had nothing to wear for two days. I met a German woman who showed me around Barbados and helped me to contact the airlines to get my luggage back. When the luggage finally came I had to leave for St. Vincent at three O'clock in the morning so I slept in the airport on top of my luggage.

My hotel as well as my visit to the Black Carib communities had already been arranged. Each day I traveled back and forth to Sandy Bay or Owia, about six miles from the city. Most of the time, the bus didn't come so I thumbed a ride or walked.

It is extremely hot on St. Vincent. One day as I was walking, an old woman with a cooler on her head and bags in her hand said, "Child, you need to slow down. You will get really tired and fall out." Not only did I accept the common sense of her advice, it was part of my training as a child growing up in Birmingham to obey adults. Slowing my pace, I walked along with her.

The same willingness of the people to participate in the study that I experienced during my previous visit had not changed. By the time I reached the third home not only did a willing respondent greet me, but also one who already knew the questions. Amazing, I thought, as this happened repeatedly. I began to wonder if people listened at the windows.

One day after an interview a woman gave me a banana. After that, people wanted to give me something everywhere I went. I tried to refuse but I could see that that wasn't appropriate so I had to accept even raw eggs. Coconut juice, a national drink, was a big offering. It wasn't coconut milk, or anything like it and I hated it. But every time someone offered it, I had to drink it with a smile.

The people seemed to always know how to get in touch with me, no matter where I was. I could be walking or on the back of a truck and I would get messages from the nurse who helped me meet people. It was comforting to know that people were watching out for me.

I also went to a Black Carib community in the extreme north, a place called Fancy. When I told someone that I was going there they looked at me as if I was crazy. A treacherous trip, to get to it you had to go up a steep cliff. If something happened to the brakes, that was it. I went up on an old bus that was packed with people and chickens. At points along the ride everyone grew quiet — the driver needed all of his concentration to maneuver the hazardous road. I could see that everyone, myself included, prayed the brakes wouldn't fail.

Arriving, I stayed with the nurse who had the only electricity in town, so people would bring things by to put in the refrigerator. At night you could still see because the moon was so bright.

I went crabbing up a mountain with the women. In the field, like the women, I always wore a skirt. While I'm an American, and they know we do things differently, they will be patient with you and help you learn the culture. I did not want to offend them by wearing pants.

They would sing as we moved up the mountain turning over rocks to find crabs. They were extremely happy with their lives although they didn't have anything. After a while I began to wonder about this. I don't think I knew as many people in the states with all the luxuries America provides who were as happy as the people in Fancy.

A lot of Pentecostal and Jesus Christ oriented groups resided in Fancy. After working during the early part of the day either in the fields, fishing or crabbing, everybody went to church at night, so I went, too. One night I didn't go to church and the next day everyone asked me where I was. There was a lot of pressure to attend church.

Lynn, the nurse, was baptized while I was there. During the service someone started talking in tongues, something I had never seen before. At one point, so caught up in the service, I felt that I was sinner and didn't deserve to be there.

The feeling was so poignant and powerful that I thought about jumping out of the window. Fortunately, the service was soon over. When I finally went down the mountain and had a couple of beers, I was over the sinner thing.

Leaving the Americas, I discovered quite disconcertingly a universal dislike for people of African ancestry. It wasn't just Whites in America, but America certainly contributed to the disdain, undoubtedly through the mass media. It wasn't just a natural human expression of ethnocentricity, whereby one race or group inherently believes it is better than another, which could suggest that racism was inevitable. The pie, or economics is an extension, intricately wrapped around racism, as the pie is only so large that people want the biggest slice for themselves and consequently, come up with reasons why others (us) should only get a very small slice. This rationale gives merit to age old wisdom that racism was not merely a socio-political weapon, but an economical one, as well. The physical form was just an identifier of economic and political status.

When I returned from Panama I came late so my friend didn't pick me up and I had to take a cab. What a hassle. Nigerian taxi cab drivers would not take me. The cabs were lined up and I got into one. To my utter astonishment, he took my luggage out and claimed that he could not take me. He told the Black female manager that I wanted to pay with a credit card, which was a lie. Then three other Nigerian also would not take me, although I was in line before a number of White families. They wanted to take the Whites because they thought they would make more money with them.

It is not just the Whites that discriminate against us, but we learn from them to do the same thing. In anthropology it is called *hegemony*[2] where you internalize the racist beliefs of the dominant population. Others do this, too. Blacks as thought of as drug dealers and pimps, while Whites are seen as police officers (a lot of this has to do with television).

In my "Race" course, some students tested this theory, interviewing Korean students. One Korean interviewee thought all Blacks were criminals. When he enrolled at UH they gave him a Black roommate. His parents called everyday to see if he was okay. He said he was afraid to go to sleep at night. One night he detoured and walked around the edge of campus because one Black guy was walking behind him. After he got to know his roommate, he stopped worrying about it. The students in my class interviewed a number of international students and there seemed to be a consensus that before meeting Blacks in the states they believed that Blacks were criminals, drug users and dealers and pimps.

This is how the world views us and what they think unless they have first-hand interaction, which many do no get. It reveals that racism is not a fact of life, but rather that it has been exported around the world through the media and that's power.

Trip to Africa (Cameroon and Central African Republic) in the Summer of
1989

I traveled from Houston to Paris where I spent a few days with a friend from
Houston, Saundra, who was vacationing there. A Moroccan friend of ours, Ha-
jib, was also in Paris, and he squired us around. It was through them that I met a
guy from Somalia. We talked about Africa and the animosity between people in
Senegal (Black) and Mauritania (Arab). People from Mauritania migrate to
Senegal, but they send them back because they're Arabs.

We went to dinner at Hajib friend house, Pat and his wife, Jewel, and their
daughter. Late that night, around 3:00 in the morning really, Hajib got Patrick
to take me home. It quickly proved to be a bad idea, with disaster written all
over the experience. Pat tried to take me to the woods to rape me.

I first became suspicious when he asked me to put my seat belt on. He also
asked me to roll up the window, but it was drizzling so that didn't seem unusual. As he drove pass a café and a number of other buildings and sites, I
hadn't seen before, I tried to ask him why we were going this way. He gestured
he didn't understand me. That he only spoke French, which I knew was true
from dinner with his family. Spotting, the Chateau, a magnificent castle that I
planned to visit, was when I definitely knew something was wrong. My hotel
was nowhere near that castle.

It wasn't until I saw the woods and a sign pointed to Paris in the other direction that I became upset. Then, when he steered the car off the road onto pave-
ment next to the woods I panicked. I tried to undo the seat belt, but couldn't.
Then I began to cry. Even though I couldn't believe this was happening, still in
the back of my mind was the thought that maybe I was being paranoid. I let him
know I didn't believe him and got out of the car. He said something to me in
French, and while I didn't know what, it instilled a sense of assurance, and I
thought, Okay I'm being paranoid and this isn't really happening.

He drove a few more yards and then turned into a country club. More woods
lay behind the club. At this point, I jumped out of the moving vehicle and ran
toward a taxi driver. The top of the taxi was dirty and I gestured wildly. Drawing pictures on top of a dirty car I told him what had happened. I wasn't even in
Paris anymore! This taxi driver took me to the hotel while Pat watched. I told
Hajib who told Pat's wife what happened, but of course she couldn't believe it,
and didn't. Hajib and Pat however, are no longer friends.

The next day I went to the Louvre. The building is a work of art. I toured it
all day and ran into one of my students from Houston. While on the escalator, I
heard someone say, "Hey, Dr. Hutchinson." I waived. I had dinner with Saundra, Hajib and a guy I met on the plane from LA, named Tim. Hajib took us to a
Moroccan restaurant where I had couscous, like a stew with millet, which was
very good. After dinner, around 11:45 p.m. we walked up Champs Le Elyssie
and saw the Arc de Tromphe. The next few days I went to Sacre Coure, a very

impressive church overlooking Paris. I also went to the Moulin Rouge, the Latin Quarters which is like the French Quarters, Notre Dame, Eiffel Tower, Pompidou Center, Hotel de Ville, Les Halles (my favorite place because it's beautiful and comfortable with a lot of cafes) and had beer or café (coffee) in any number of the outside restaurants.

I took the plane to Yaoundé, Cameroon but as usual things didn't go well. I was going to setup a study on HIV and condom use. The plane was late, I missed my connection, so I had to spend the night in Doula. It took me a while to realize that I was in the Motherland. By the time I woke up, the first van to the airport had left, as had the first flight to Yaoundé.

The airport in Yaoundé was chaotic with people pulling on my luggage and taxi drivers trying to get me to ride with them. Two taxi drivers almost fought over who would take me to the hotel. After having lunch in the hotel I wanted to go to the bank and the people in the hotel advised taking a taxi. Well, the bank was right around the corner and when I got there it was closed.

I met an administrator from the World Health Organization (WHO) along with a representative from Save the Children who had come to educate people about condoms. Dining with them, along with a professor from the university and some other doctors, we ate chicken, porcupine and pignant (a cross between an anteater and armadillo). Interesting, it had a rather gamy taste.

One night we went to the Kavou, a hot club in town. There were a lot of White men and Indians there. Some of the Black Africans don't like to go there because of the White men. I can see their point. They were like slimy vultures preying on young girls. They did the Makossa and then another dance where they moved the middle part of their body extremely fast. People were standing around them as they did it two at a time. We left around two am and there were prostitutes being picked up about a half block from my hotel.

The news in Yaoundé was interesting. They discussed an alligator had bitten a part of a woman's body and they couldn't keep blood in her. In another story a woman punished her son for transforming into a demon. The problem was she couldn't find him at night because of the transformation. It's believed he roamed the village nightly hurting people.

I met a traditional healer who heals fractures with oils from pythons and chickens. They rub the oil on the arm, and then wrap it with chicken and some other kinds of bone around it. The chief of medical services lives like a king. He has a house in an upper class neighborhood and a villa in the woods outside Yaoundé.

I met Leezy, the wife of a former student of mine. She never told me she was an MD. Leezy and Larry were married in the traditional way with palm oil poured over her naked body. Her mother was a princess, and her family was part of royalty in Bamenda. We had a green vegetable with dough like bread. They put palm oil on everything. Again, I didn't like the palm oil or the vegetable. As I got to know Leezy, I realized what a dog Larry is. He wanted to control her, but she is not that kind of person. During a six-year period Larry only sent her $1,000. With two kids to feed, clothe, and educate that was nothing. Besides he received over $12,000 for land the government bought, but he wanted her to put it in an account with only his name. He didn't even offer her more money.

There are different areas for different things in the market, like jewelry or leather. While at the jewelry, a White guy came by in a car and told a guy to tell me he wanted to talk to me. It was easy to see how girls could be turned into prostitutes. Not because they wanted to, but because in a poor country a guy comes by with money, offering a temporary way out of poverty.

We went to a chicken parlor, a restaurant (some are fish parlors). It's a restaurant in a woman's house. Leezy said only women who are single, not with their husband, would have a place like this (when women leave their husband, they must also leave their children, for children belong to the father). Leezy said you have to know the people running the parlor because someone could pay them extra to slip poison into your drink. At the hospital she sees people who have been poisoned by venom or poisonous plants. She told me about the *Junking* that she belongs to. Obviously not junking as we know it, either trashing useless stuff or visiting thrift shops, auctions, and the like. Rather, it's similar to an investment club where each member contributes 55,000 francs, and at the end of the year or after six (6) months, one person collects the money from the other twelve members. Women in the market do it on a weekly basis. Prostitutes even have their own Junking. If a prostitute has a boyfriend and she doesn't pay her part she is fined for not making the boyfriend pay. She pays because she wants to be part of the Junking.

There are social benefits to be derived, as well. For instance, if someone has a death in the family, they receive money free of charge from the Junking. Roughly ten percent, for example 5,000 of the 55,000 francs is used for emergencies for members. During the year, they loan out the money, so they collect interest. All of this is divided between the members. That's one reason the banking industry is in such bad shape. Every responsible person is a member of a Junking. People don't like to go to the bank because they may not be able to get their money out.

Peter, a researcher in Yaoundé, and I set out for Ebolowa, about a two-hour trek through the bush. Drawn there because of the high HIV rate, we were accompanied by two medical students to help with collecting blood samples.

The bush is thick like a jungle. It's noisy from the birds and monkey screeching and while not overhanging like the Amazon, it has a lot of trees and tall bushes and grasses. It was not as hot as I expected, probably because of the shade provided by the trees. Everything was green or had colorful large flowers that I had never seen before. It was beautiful and scary at the same time. Along the way, we stumbled across two guys who were trying to sell two guenon monkeys (used for food, as pets, and in medical research) for 3500 Francs.

Our destination was farther than we expected, so we checked into a hotel. The room was okay, but the water was brown. That night I had Cervett, a member of the cat family, for dinner; it tasted gamy as you might expect. We visited Peter's sister, who is married to a doctor; servants tend their family. This is really a class-oriented society.

I met a woman over the child survivorship program that said the people were not concerned about AIDS. They believed it was something the White man invented to stop them from practicing polygamy and *Copin* (a lot of girlfriends). I helped Peter with his study by asking demographic questions while he collected blood samples.

That night we went to Bambu village where the upper class hangs out. Then we went to club Katousse. They played American, Cameroonian and reggae music. The club could have existed anywhere in the states.

Peter, one of the medical students, and I got malaria while we were in Ebolowa. Since I had been taking my malaria pills, my case wasn't as bad as Peter's. It affected his brain. Evidently there's nothing unusual about getting malaria although you've taken the medication properly. I stayed in bed for three days. The third night Leezy wanted to go out but I told her I'm too sick. She gave me some syrup like concoction that made me feel better, but I still didn't think I should party. The fourth day I was able to walk around a little.

I went to Bamenda with Leezy to meet her family. On the way we bought a guenon monkey for 2500 Francs. Bamenda is colder than Yaoundé because it is situated in the mountains, a more savanna like region whereas Yaoundé is forested. Leezy always brings things home for all of the relatives. She doesn't make much money and has two kids, but because she's an MD, they think she can do everything. It's real hard on her. Her cousin had died two weeks ago, so we said a prayer at the edge of his grave. Her aunt took the boy to a traditional healer who treated him, but he died anyway. The healer said her husband's relatives killed the boy (poison or something). Leezy said the symptoms sounded like renal disease. If Leezy had not visited now the aunt would have thought that she didn't visit because she killed the boy. So Leezy had to visit. In addition to visiting all of her relatives, she had to visit her husband's relatives, for the wife belongs to the husband's family.

We went to the Fon's (the Chief) Palace where we met her sister-in-law. We had to take off our shoes when we entered the Fon's reception area and stand when he came into the room. We couldn't speak until after he had spoken. Women have to talk in a whisper with their hands clasped before their mouth. If a man pays a fine, he can clap and talk to the Fon before he speaks. He asked me a lot of questions about my family, the United States, politics, and Jesse Jackson. I enjoyed talking to him. He realizes that change is necessary. For instance, that they should have smaller families but the problem is how to do that. Leezy's sister-in-law ran off to Nigeria because she didn't want to marry the Fon. But they went there and forced her to return.

On the way home in a van with a number of people, we stopped a lot, suffering through two flat tires. The driver was up to no good because he tried to take me home last. We weren't too far from my hotel and Leezy told him where to take me but he wouldn't. He dropped the others off. Before, he had been driving fast and now all of a sudden, he was driving slow. He acted suspicious, and a little voice warned me that this was bad. I followed it and got out with Leezy. She took a cab with me to my place and the same driver brought her back to her place.

After spending a month in Cameroon, I left for Bangui, Central African Republic to check out the feasibility of doing a study there. The flight from Doula to Bangui was supposed to leave at 7 pm, but didn't leave until 2 am the next morning. You just have to relax and go with the flow.

Bangui is really the bush. You can walk a few feet and you're in the jungle. The city itself is really the bush. People either live well or are extremely poor. Mainly poverty existed here in Bangui.

When I arrived at the Pasteur Institute I found out the person that the director said would help me (the director who I corresponded with was out of the country) knew nothing about my proposal or project. At 7:30 in the morning, I was trying to get him interested in the project. After about an hour, he was convinced and gave me a little house on the premises with a bedroom, living room, kitchen and bathroom. As I talked with him about the project, I found out that people were going on holiday and the people I needed to talk to may not be in town. I got an interpreter (who wanted to charge 1000 Francs a minute, but we had to come to a different agreement on that) and introduced myself to Dr. Somse who was over the Program SIDA.

The French at the Pasteur Institute didn't know anything about the people. They stayed in the compound, a fortress, their servants bought their food, and they worked and played inside the fortress. The people in the community don't like the French, especially the people at the Pasteur Institute but put up with them because it is the only hospital. The French practiced a racism that resembled that of the Old South in America. One day while having lunch with the assistant director, he started talking about the food. I didn't understand what brought this conversation on. He was looking at me and talking. As it turned out, he was actually talking to the servant, but he didn't look at him when he talked to him. He just talked and the guy did what he wanted. It was like the worker (I hate calling him a servant) was not a real person.

People eat centipedes here. In the market the centipedes are in a mound like a mound of potatoes or tomatoes. They're brown worm-like insects, with a lot of Black in their coloring. I don't know what could be nutritious about centipedes, but it is the national soup and everyone eats it. The women are constantly grabbing the centipedes as they try to run away. I passed on the soup, thank-you.

That night I stood on the sink to watch the people in the back yard. Looking down, I noticed a curved Black thing. Foolishly, I jumped off the sink to the side and ran outside to get someone. Luckily a guy was working outside and I got him and another guy to kill it. I think it was a pretty nasty snake because they were afraid of it too. After that I was afraid to get up at night, and I always made sure my mosquito net was snug under the mattress.

I visited a number of places and met the representative of USAID, a biologist before he became a diplomat. I also met an anthropologist at the Universite de Bangui. I had to fill out an application to do research in Bangui. They didn't have the forms, but promised to deliver them when they did find them.

As you can see, even the best-laid plans go awry when conducting research in the field. Stays are necessarily lengthy as to glean better insight into the particular society, regardless of the nature of the study. We must learn the "whys" and "hows" of the people's customs and beliefs in order to better serve them, as well as fulfill the purpose of the study. This cannot be accomplished in a few short weeks.

The benefits of fieldwork outweigh the downsides—contracting a life-threatening illness, running into people of ill reproach, having to re-sell your idea, and even finding a snake in your residence (smile). The purpose of the study aside, the wealth of knowledge that cannot be found in a book is plenty enough reward. Additionally, the potential of developing lifelong friendships is real, with the added bonus of establishing a network of useful contacts should the data suggest the necessity of a follow-up.

No, things don't always go according to plan, but neither does life. And like in life, one recovers, adjusts, and keep going because the goal is more important than the obstacles and hassles.

Conclusion

Evolvement

"Who are you?"

Power, Race and Culture: the Evolution of a Black Anthropologist evolved from a general feeling that I've seen more racism than anybody. Like a shadow, it has dogged my path from the personal experiences growing up in Birmingham, Alabama to my educational training and subsequent professional pursuits. There is no doubt that I've seen racism in the thousands of bones I examined, revealing improper nutrition and poor health care because the patients were of the wrong color. It resided in the halls of academia where the perpetuation of untruths were promulgated in spite of evidence to the contrary that Blacks are genetically inferior. And, it continues in my professional pursuits where Black concerns are deemed the purview of Blacks only. All represent denials that can be traced back to racism.

It has been unending, and undeniable. There is nothing serendipitous about the tons of data that show the collusive course history took in the direction of race and power. It reveals the absurdities Black culture has had to deal with 24-7, for nearly 400 years. We were allowed baptism in the master's faith, but a freed body didn't come with the newly cleansed soul. Although physically free, Jim Crow restrained us. Receiving Civil Rights, Blacks were forced to litigate to actualize them; allowed an education, but through inferior schools, to cite a few of the racial incidents that make our "equality" meaningless.

Whenever we walk down the street we race people, performing an informal form of profiling. We focus on their physical appearance such as skin color, hair texture, and eye color and place them into racial categories. The person spied is either Black, White, some type of Hispanic/Latino or Asian: there is no room in our collective consciousness for Other.

Evidence of this can be seen in the census as the bureau has intermittently created additional categories in which to place people. Individuals can now check Middle Eastern and a variety of Asian categories. There continues to be the belief that physical form can be placed into discrete categories, although we know that no one is an average. No one has the combination of traits, outward and inward (such as genes and biochemical makeup) that allows them to be placed into a discrete racial group. In particular, the Human Genome Project has shown—as we've known since the eighteenth century—that we are more similar than different. All variation overlaps, and there are no qualitative differences between what we call racial groups. In other words, any trait that you can think of is found in all populations. Only the frequency of the trait varies by population.

We have always known that races do not exist in nature only variation. Yet, we continue to try to put that variation into discrete groups. Why? Because we think there are mental, emotional, and behavioral traits that correlate with those discrete categories. When we walk down the street and race people, we also assume we know something about that person. We think, for instance, that we know the type of music they like, the foods they eat, or the type of community that they live in.

Since the beginning of the race concept, around the 1500s, it was believed that culture is determined by biology. Consequently, outward appearance became the yardstick against which cultural achievement or level of civilization was measured. Those in power determined who possessed or lacked civilization. Culture was then determined to be belief systems, values and behavior that Europeans possessed. Others lacked culture or were considered savages or barbarians. So they determined what physical form went along with culture.

Today, we know that culture is learned behavior. It is not biologically based. You learn your culture during the maturation and socialization processes. Everyone is born into a culture, learning what is appropriate for that culture. You may learn about computers or you may learn how to track an antelope and find water holes. Whatever you need to learn to survive, you do so through your culture as all cultures help its members to survive. If they didn't, the people and that culture would cease to exist.

Even though the difference between culture and race are constantly taught, they are habitually connected despite a wealth of knowledge to the contrary. Why? Because we have racial identities, we think of ourselves in racial terms. We grow up and are socialized to identify with "our" group, people who look and behave like us. In this socialization process we learn the values and behaviors that go along with the group and each generation, then, it appears that cultural patterns are tied to physical form. We internalize this belief as we learn our culture, and in the process, develop identities that focus on race as an important integrating characteristic. We rally around this identity in social movements and celebrations such as festivals. This reinforces our racial identities and continues the belief that culture and physical form are intertwined. If someone deviates from the pattern, they are either the exception or pushed into a category.

Our skin color precedes us into any room. We are measured by it and instantly deemed suspect by others. To us, our identity is reflective of a test question where the wrong answer results in a lost opportunity—job, fair housing, education, et cetera. The grade reflects, however, that neither a wrong nor right answer is correct in reality. Our problem suggests that we have misinterpreted the data (using their interpretations instead of reaching our own conclusions), which is traceable to being historically ungrounded, hence, the resurfacing of the question—"Who am I?"

Who we perceive ourselves to be has always played a major role in how we live our lives. For example, if we perceive ourselves as generous, even though inherently stingy, our generosity is manifested in a gift we bestow. And how we perceive our Blackness is dependent upon how we answer the question of our ancestry: are we the descendants of ex-slaves or enslaved Africans?

Blackness is how people of African ancestry think about their heritage. Some view themselves as the descendants of ex-slaves. For them, moving up the class hierarchy, assimilation into mainstream society and breaking the glass ceiling are signs of success or equality. They might be called followers of Booker T. Washington. It's apparent that some Blacks seek assimilation and class climbing (not saying that upward mobility is bad). However, to do it while saying that race and racism are not issues is to keep your head buried in the sand. Having White friends, being in a relationship with a person of another ethnicity or being financially or occupationally successful may suggest to them that racism is not a limiting factor. 'I did it on my own and you can too.'

Maybe these are the new Black republicans who fight for the rights of big business to oppress employees. I have talked to students who don't think that their White friends can be racist because if they were they wouldn't be friends with them. This occurred with one student who joined a predominately White student organization. At first he thought the members really wanted his participation. But he soon found that they simply wanted to taunt him as their Black member, to show that they are liberal and diverse. When it came to key positions on committees, he was not told about meetings and was excluded from the decision-making hierarchy. These ex-slaves often have a rude awakening and find that they are alone without the network of community to socially and emotionally provide support for them.

Others consider themselves descendants of enslaved Africans. This approach might represent followers of W.E.B DuBois. There are a variety of ways that such individuals think of themselves. For instance, there is the Afrocentric group that attempts to approach American life through an African-centered heritage. There is a celebration of Kwanzaa, adoption of African names, wearing of African clothing and an attempt to emulate what they consider African ways of thinking. The problem with this approach is that Africa is a continent with diverse cultures. No one culture, no one way of doing can be used to represent

"Africa." Additionally, the borrowing of individual items does not result in a cohesive way of living. It just means you do this or that, for there is no holistic approach to life with a particular way of thinking. Do Africans in America want to adopt "all" characteristics or behavior patterns found in African societies? If no, how do we decide which ones to adopt?

This raises a question for people of African ancestry. What is our racial identity? Is it as an enslaved African or ex-slave? Being an African in America means being varied and inclusive of perspectives. It is a type of Creolization of the Black experience in America. There is no need to pick one or the other because we are both. On the one hand, we have been freed from the severe oppression of our ancestors; yet, we continue the struggle of our ancestors as enslaved Africans in America.

One only needs to look around to see that communities of Black people in urban areas, called ghettoes, are another manifestation of plantation life. The poverty, poor health care, and crowded living conditions mimic the life of slaves on plantations. Beatings of Black men by police officers who are not punished continue the slave code where masters could legitimately inflict violence on their slaves. Unlike Whites, slaves did not receive benefits from a legal system that was designed to protect the innocent as well as punish the guilty. As a matter of fact, slaves were often punished more severely than Whites for the same crimes. The disproportional use of the death penalty for Blacks compared to Whites exemplifies this continued pattern.

Slavery for Blacks in the United States is a matter of degree. Ex-slave is one extreme; enslaved African is another point on the continuum that is complicated by our Americanism. This was shown in the event of September 11 where Blacks, like other Americans, eagerly showed their patriotism by waving the American flag and endorsing the pulling back of human rights such as freedom of movement and being held by the legal system without being accused of a crime. Americans rallied around "Homeland Defense", and had an "us versus them" perspective although the same America that they were praising would beat them for a minor traffic violation, torture and sodomize them (as in the New York case), overcharge them for insurance (as we're finding in efforts to receive reparations), deny them decent housing, an education, and equal employment.

The life of Africans in America is not a matter of ex-slave versus enslaved African. It's about adapting the African experience to American life and in the process producing African Americans. A group with one foot in America and another on the homeland that come together to create something completely new, African Americans.

Blackness is a connection to ancestry that is as diverse as the ethnicities of our ancestors who came to these shores over 400 years ago. I do not think of myself as Afrocentric because that is a broad statement that is unclear, poorly defined, and whose meaning usually indicates a list of particular expectations. I think of myself as Black-centered. Being Black-centered is inclusive of the "African" (varied experiences), as well as African-American experiences. It includes the corporate woman, dreadlocked man, maid, teacher, and writer. It is inclusive of the varied ways of living and thinking among all Black Americans. For me, Blackness is about commitment to community, family, and heritage. It is about remembering the past but not wallowing in it. It is a celebration of the past and not a continual reason for my misfortune. Blackness is ancestry and the unity derived from fighting a common oppression that attempts to subordinate Blackness to third-class life throughout the world. It is a commitment to improving the quality of life of people with African heritage and all oppressed people.

My becoming an anthropologist is due to the history of my childhood and the history of America. In this history race was a salient, invasive, encompassing factor that affected my family, my education, and my community. Race segregated us and created a secure village life with solidarity against a common enemy. Simultaneously, it forced me to look at human variation and the social landscape that made physical features important in American life. At a young age, through family and community, I could see the impact of race on the lives of the people around me. Growing up in Birmingham during the civil rights period I could also see that those in power used physical variation for social, political, and economic reasons, the White dominate population, to maintain access to valued resources (education, good health and housing). In other words, the control of power produced good living conditions for those with power, Whites, and poor living conditions for others. I knew through community and attending a predominately White high school that physical features that were the impetus for some Whites to bomb and lynch Blacks were not related to intelligence or moral or behavioral factors. Their connection was to maintain segregation, a caste system with Blacks at the bottom and privilege and access to wealth and power for Whites. It was not really about biology. It was about maintaining privilege. Before I became an anthropologist I already knew what race was and what it was not.

My training in anthropology filled in the details of this scenario from an historical and biological perspective through the study of living and dead people. In this scenario I learned theories derived from White beliefs of Black inferiority and how these beliefs were used to create political and economic policies that perpetuated these beliefs. It was a circular process made possible through the power of the dominant group to control knowledge and the educational system. In this way race was made real and racism was promulgated through the whole process. In essence, anthropology taught me why we think about groups of people in the way that we do.

'Outting' racism first requires knowing who you are and where you came from. That this his-story has been imposed on us with devastating effects does not warrant the suicide, figurative and literal, that we commit daily. Knowing who we are is the only inoculation to a surefire extinction.

Notes and References

1. The Environmental Protection Agency defines environmental justice as fair and meaningful inclusion of people regardless of color, race, national origin, or income in the development, implementation and enforcement of laws related to environmental regulations and policies (www.epa.gov/compliance/environmentaljustice/).
2. Hegemony occurs in stratified societies when subordinates conform to the dominate group by internalizing its values and accepting the naturalness of the social order (Kottak, 2004).

Alvarez, Robert. 1994. "Un Chilero en la Academia: Sifting, Shifting, and the Recruitment of Minorities in Anthropology." In: *Race*. S. Gregory and R. Sanjek (eds). Pp 257-69. Rutgers University Press: New Brunswick, New Jersey.

Bell, Bernard and E. Grosholz. 1996. *W.E.B. DuBois on Race and Culture: Philosophy, Politics, and Poetics*. New York: Routledge.

Bowen, William G. and D. Bok. 1998. *The Shape of the River: Long-Term Consequences of Considering Race in College and University Admissions*. Princeton, NJ: Princeton University Press.

Comstock, G.W. 1957. "An Epidemiological Study of Blood Pressure Levels in a Biracial Community in the Southern U.S." American Journal of Hygiene 65:271-315.

Cooper, R., and R. David. 1986. "The Biological Concept of Race and its Application to Public Health and Epidemiology." Journal Health Political Policy Law 11:97-116.

D'Angelo, Raymond. 2001. *The American Civil Rights Movement: Readings and Interpretations*. New York: McGraw-Hill/Dushkin.

Drake, St. Clair and Horace Cayton. 1945. *Black Metropolis: A Study of Negro Life in a Northern City*. Vol 2. New York: Harcourt, Brace.

Frazier, E. Franklin. 1969. *The Negro Church in America*. New York: Schocken Books, Inc.

Geronimus, A.T. 1992. "The Weathering Hypothesis and the Health of African-American Women and Infants: Evidence and Speculation." Ethnicity and Disease 2:207-221.

———.1996. "Black/White Differences in the Relationship of Maternal Age to Birthweight: A Population-Based Test of the Weathering Hypothesis." Social Science and Medicine 42(4):589-97.

Birthweight: A Population-Based Test of the Weathering Hypothesis." Social Science and Medicine 42(4):589-97.

Goodman, A. 2000. "Why Genes Don't Count (for Racial Differences in Health)." American Journal of Public Health 90(11):1699-1701.

Hill, H. and J.E. Jones. 1993. *Race in America: the Struggle for Equality*. Madison, Wisconsin.: University of Wisconsin Press.

Hutchinson, Janice Faye. 1979. *A Study of Biological Relationships between Archaic and Mississippian Skeletal Populations in Northern Alabama*. Master's Thesis. University of Alabama.

Hutchinson, Janice Faye. 1984. *A Biocultural Analysis of Blood Pressure Variation among the Black Caribs and Creoles of St. Vincent, West Indies*. Dissertation. University of Kansas.

Hutchinson, J. 1986. "The Relationship Between African Admixture and Blood Pressure Variation in the Caribbean." Human Heredity, 36:12-18.

Hutchinson, Janis and Michael H. Crawford. 1981. "Genetic Determinants of Blood Pressure Levels Among the Black Caribs of St. Vincent." Human Biology, 53: 453-66.

Jones, C.P., T.A. LaVeist, and M. Lillie-Blanton. 1991. "'Race' In The Epidemiologic Literature: An Examination of the American Journal of Epidemiology, 1921-1990.' American Journal of Epidemiology 134(10):1079-1084.

Kaminer, B. and W.P.W. Lutz. 1960. "Blood Pressure in Bushmen of the Kalahari Desert." Circulation 22:289-295.

Klineberg, O. 1935. *Negro Intelligence and Selective Migration*. New York: Columbia University Press

Kottak, Conrad. 2004. *Anthropology: The Exploration of Human Diversity*. New York: McGraw-Hill.

Krieger, N. and M. Bassett. 1986. "The Health of Black Folk: Disease, Class and Ideology in Science." Monthly Review 38:74-85.

Loewen. James W. 1999. *Lies Across America: What our Historic Sites Get Wrong*. New York: New Press.

Marable, Manning. 2000. *How Capitalism Underdeveloped Black America*. Cambridge, Ma.: South End Press.

Marriott, Michel. 1991. Essence (November):118.

Morrison, Toni. 1994. *The Bluest Eye*. New York : Plume Book.

Morton, S.G. 1844. *Crania Aegyptica: Observations on Egyptian Ethnography, derived from Anatomy, History, and the Monuments*. Philadelphia: John Penington.

Murray, C. and R.J. Herrnstein. 1994. *The Bell Curve: Intelligence and Class Structure in American life*. New York : Free Press.

Nobles, M.2000. History Counts: A Comparative Analysis of Racial/Color Categorization in US and Brazilian Censuses. American Journal of Public Health 90(11): 1738-45.

Pollitzer, William S. 1999. *The Gullah People and Their African Heritage*. Athens, Ga: University of Georgia Press.

Quarles, Benjamin. 1969. *The Negro in the Making of America*. New York: Collier Books.

Russell, Kathy, Midge Wilson, and Ronald Hall. 1992. *The Color Complex: The Politics of Skin Color among African Americans*. New York: Harcourt Brace Jovanovich Publishers.

Rice, G. 1972. "The Curse That Never Was (Genesis 9:18-27)." The Journal of Religious Thought 29:5-27.

Smedley, Audrey .1999. *Race in North America: Origin and Evolution of a Worldview.* Boulder, Colorado: Westview Press.

Smitherman, Geneva. 1977. *Talkin and Testifyin: The Language of Black America.* Detroit, Mi.: Wayne State University Press.

Stocking, George W. 1982. *Race, Culture, and Evolution: Essays in the History of Anthropology.* Chicago, IL: The University of Chicago Press.

Williams, A.W. 1969. "Blood Pressure Differences in Kikuyu and Samburu Communities in Kenya." East African Medical Journal 46:262-72.

Wohl, Alexander. 2001. "Diversity on Trial." American Prospect 12(8):37-39.

Author Biographical Sketch

Janis Faye Hutchinson, Ph.D., M.P.H. is a biological/medical anthropologist in the Department of Anthropology, University of Houston. She received my doctorate from the University of Kansas; and my master's and bachelor degrees from the University of Alabama. Her research interests include condom use, HIV/AIDS, racism and health, and health issues among minority populations. Her publications focus on these topics and African-American identity as shown in *Cultural Portrayals of African Americans: Creating an Ethnic/Racial Identity*, 1997. Currently she is examining the impact of recent DNA information (mapping of the human genome) on health beliefs among Indian/Hindu Americans.

Index

www.ingramcontent.com/pod-product-compliance
Lightning Source LLC
Chambersburg PA
CBHW021822270326
41932CB00007B/295